just

THE
JOB

Leisure, Sport
& Entertainment

*Also published in the **Just the Job!** series:*

Leisure, Sport
& Entertainment

Lifetime Careers
WILTSHIRE

Hodder & Stoughton

A MEMBER OF THE HODDER HEADLINE GROUP

Just the Job! draws directly on the CLIPS careers information database developed and maintained by Lifetime Careers Wiltshire and used by almost every careers service in the UK. The database is revised annually using a rigorous update schedule and incorporates material collated through desk/telephone research and information provided by all the professional bodies, institutions and training bodies with responsibility for course accreditation and promotion of each career area.

ISBN 0 340 68775 4
First published 1997

Impression number	10	9	8	7	6	5	4	3	2	1
Year	2002	2001	2000	1999	1998	1997				

Printed in Great Britain for Hodder & Stoughton Educational, the educational publishing division of Hodder Headline Plc, 338 Euston Road, London NW1 3BH, by Cox & Wyman Ltd, Reading, Berkshire.

CONTENTS

JUST THE JOB!

The *Just the Job!* series ranges over the entire spectrum of occupations and is intended to generate job ideas and stretch horizons of interest and possibility, allowing you to explore families of jobs for which you might have appropriate ability and aptitude. Each *Just the Job!* book looks in detail at a popular area or type of work, covering:

- ways into work;
- essential qualifications;
- educational and training options;
- working conditions;
- progression routes;
- potential career portfolios.

The information given in *Just the Job!* books is detailed and carefully researched. Obvious bias is excluded to give an even-handed picture of the opportunities available, and course details and entry requirements are positively checked in an annual update cycle by a team of careers information specialists. The text is written in approachable, plain English, with a minimum of technical terms.

In Britain today, there is no longer the expectation of a career for life, but support has increased for life-long learning and the acquisition of skills which will help young and old to make sideways career moves – perhaps several times during a working life – as well as moving into work carrying higher levels of responsibility and reward. *Just the Job!* invites you to select an appropriate direction for your *own* career progression.

Educational and vocational qualifications

A level – Advanced level of the General Certificate of Education

AS level – Advanced Supplementary level of the General Certificate of Education (equivalent to half an A level)

BTEC – Business and Technology Education Council: awards qualifications such as BTEC First, BTEC National Certificate/Diploma, etc

GCSE – General Certificate of Secondary Education

GNVQ/GSVQs – General National Vocational Qualification/ General Scottish Vocational Qualification: awarded at Foundation, Intermediate and Advanced levels by BTEC, City & Guilds, Royal Society of Arts and SQA

HND/C – BTEC Higher National Diploma/Certificate

International Baccalaureate – recognised by all UK universities as equivalent to a minimum of two A levels

NVQ/SVQs – National/Scottish Vocational Qualifications

PGCE – Postgraduate Certificate in Education

SCE – Scottish Certificate of Education, at **Standard** Grade (equate directly with GCSEs: grades 1–3 in SCEs at Standard Grade are equivalent to GCSE grades A–C) and **Higher** Grade (equate with the academic level attained after one year of a two-year A level course: three to five Higher Grades are broadly equivalent to two to four A levels at grades A–E)

Vocational work-based credits	NVQ/SVQ level 1	NVQ/SVQ level 2	NVQ/SVQ level 3	NVQ/SVQ level 4
Vocational qualifications: *a mix of theory and practice*	Foundation GNVQ/ GSVQ; BTEC First	Intermediate GNVQ/GSVQ	Advanced GNVQ/GSVQ; BTEC National Diploma/Certificate	BTEC Higher National Diploma/ Certificate
Educational qualifications	GCSE/SCE Standard Grade pass grades	GCSE grades A–C; SCE Standard Grade levels 1–3	Two A levels; four Scottish Highers; Baccalaureate	University degree

INTRODUCTION

Within the arena of sport, leisure pursuits and the entertainment world, there are many and varied possibilities for finding paid employment. Not everyone can be a professional tennis player, footballer or cricketer, nor can we all hold centre stage in a Hollywood filmset or at the Royal Festival Hall, but there are many opportunities for those with interest, enthusiasm and some talent to work in jobs connected with physical training and recreational activities. You may want to assist in skills training in a one-to-one coaching situation, or teach within a group context, or choose to work in an administrative/managerial capacity in a sports or leisure centre. You may prefer to work on the health side of sporting activities, work in the field of entertainment, or use your recreational interest in therapy work.

Entry requirements vary from few, if any, qualifications to degree level.

The sections on the commercial leisure industry and careers related to sport will give you a general overview of the range of salaried occupations in the fields of leisure, sport and entertainment.

THE COMMERCIAL LEISURE INDUSTRY

The commercial leisure industry covers enterprises such as cinemas, dance-halls, casinos, nightclubs, social clubs, ice rinks, bowling alleys, amusement parks, holiday centres and leisure complexes. Jobs range from recreation assistant to general manager, and there are opportunities for those with every level of academic qualification, from just a few GCSEs to a degree or the equivalent.

The commercial leisure industry is very susceptible to change, depending on what is currently popular or fashionable. Cinemas and tenpin bowling, for instance, both suffered a decline in popularity some years ago, followed by a revival in their fortunes.

What the work involves

Work in the leisure industry involves unsocial hours, with evenings, late nights and weekends being the peak times for use of most facilities. This industry is one where you work while other people relax and enjoy themselves. Willingness to move for a job and to gain experience can be important, especially if you work for one of the large groups with operations all over the country. Non-managerial jobs may often be part-time or seasonal.

Opportunities for people under 18 may be limited, especially in places which serve alcohol and cater for an adult clientele.

Management

Many universities offer a range of degree courses in leisure and recreation management, and some offer study at postgraduate level. There is also an increasing range of courses in leisure and recreation which can provide a base for a career in management. Many schools and colleges offer GNVQs at different levels in leisure and recreation. The Institute of Leisure and Amenity Management (ILAM) offers a work-based project qualification. Large organisations, such as the Rank Organisation, offer management trainee posts.

Motivation, a head for business and job experience are keenly sought and can be more important qualifications for a post than formal training and qualifications. A confident, extrovert personality is a vital asset. Experience in the hotel and catering industry may be useful, since most commercial leisure operations offer catering facilities.

It is advisable to gain experience wherever you can – possibly through holiday or temporary employment. Often leisure organisations have a considerable need for seasonal staff during the main holiday periods, so temporary jobs may not be too difficult to find. You could look out for job vacancies in the papers, through careers services or Jobcentres, and write for information to employers in the industry, stating which areas of operation you are interested in.

Leisure operations

There are many other jobs in the leisure industry which do not require qualifications or long training. Many positions involve working with the public, such as cinema and theatre attendants, box office staff and swimming pool and sports centre attendants. For these jobs, you'll need to be good at dealing with people, and of reasonably smart appearance. Interest and enthusiasm for the leisure activities involved may help you in applying for jobs

and selling yourself at interviews. For most poolside jobs you'll be asked for lifesaving qualifications.

Holiday centres, like Warner's, Pontins or Butlins, employ people to help their clients to enjoy themselves. This sometimes involves performing or entertaining, but is largely a matter of letting people know what activities are available and encouraging them to join in. An extrovert personality, and perhaps experience working on playschemes or youth club activities, can be useful. The work is, of course, mostly seasonal.

Other jobs include clerical and financial work, computing, operating equipment, maintenance, cleaning, caretaking and catering. Lots of these jobs involve shift work and can be part-time. Many cinemas, for example, only open in the evening. Larger employers may offer chances of training and promotion. The careers service will know of any training opportunities with employers in your area.

These kinds of jobs are often advertised in local papers, in Jobcentres and by your local careers service. It is also worth going to any sports and leisure centres in your area to ask about vacancies.

LEISURE & RECREATION MANAGEMENT

L eisure is a growth industry. There are many more facilities provided for the public nowadays than there were 20 years ago. All sorts of organisations are involved in providing access to sport and leisure – local authorities, commercial organisations, industrial organisations, universities and colleges, voluntary groups and trusts. So, if you want to get into this sort of work, you'll need to be really keen, and to get the best pre-entry qualifications you can manage, both practical and academic.

Managers in the leisure and recreation industry need to be willing and able to take on a varied workload, and – like their staff – work in the evenings and at weekends when necessary.

Sporting opportunities

The Sports Council

This is an independent body which promotes sport and facilities for physical recreation in England. There are councils in Scotland, Wales and Northern Ireland which have similar responsibilities, and also regional and local sports councils to advise on more local requirements. They are staffed by research, administrative and technical personnel – but not in great numbers. Qualifications in physical education, sports science and recreation management are useful for this area of work.

National sports centres

The Sports Council runs six national sports centres, of which five are residential, with facilities for participants in top-level sport. The priority groups which they cater for are coaches, officials and national teams, but they also host events and have facilities for general and basic courses.

Management of a centre involves responsibility for its promotion and development, liaison with organisers of courses and events, accommodation booking, allocating facilities, supervision of staff, the budget, catering facilities, etc. A range of managers would be employed at a single centre. There could be opportunities for sports practitioners, people with sports science/physical education backgrounds, or those with other experience or qualifications appropriate to particular posts, for example in recreational or institutional management.

Local authority sports centres

Sports and leisure centres may have facilities for both indoor and outdoor sports. Some centres may have extensive facilities, including pools, sports halls, fitness suites, bars and eating areas – and perhaps an ice rink and arts facilities. Such a centre could employ a number of staff at supervisory and management levels. In contrast, a small local authority sports centre with a pool and dry sports facilities might have a manager working with two assistants. The manager's responsibilities would include recruiting staff, promoting events, organising advertising, managing the finances, health and safety and ensuring the smooth operation of the centre on a daily basis.

For a post involving management of swimming facilities, baths management qualifications and experience are desirable. Other sports qualifications, such as coaching, may suit 'dry' sports centre jobs.

University, college and similar sports centres

Educational establishments often provide very good sports and leisure facilities. Jobs can involve both administrative work and physical education/coaching. A physical education background is usually preferred.

And for the less sporting . . .

There are various organisations which provide non-sport outdoor leisure facilities. Opportunities range from general administrative work to very specialist jobs, such as land agency.

Outdoor holiday organisations

These include the Youth Hostels Associations, the Holiday Fellowship, the Countryside Holiday Association, and the Camping Club of Great Britain and Ireland. These organisations provide reasonably priced holiday accommodation and promote outdoor recreational activities such as walking, canoeing, pony-trekking and cycling. The Youth Hostels Association provides mainly for young people, while the other organisations cater more for families and older people. Senior posts are very few and vacancies are rare. The requirements are generally for good administrators and for specialists such as surveyors and accountants.

There are also holiday organisations which operate on a strictly commercial basis – for example PGL Adventure Holidays and Camp Beaumont. These provide activity holidays for children, teenagers and adults. There are job opportunities (including seasonal openings) for instructors and supervisors, as well as the usual administrative posts.

The National Trust & the National Trust for Scotland

Some opportunities with the National Trust can be described as leisure and recreation management, in terms of making land and properties accessible to the public. Vacancies are few – there is a low turnover of staff. Most of the senior staff are land agents and there are few jobs for people without a specialisation, such as law, land agency, estate management, marketing and/or accountancy. The National Trust for Scotland is a much smaller organisation, although broadly similar to the National Trust.

The National Parks

Quite a number of graduates work in the National Parks, though there are also posts for people with other backgrounds. However, vacancies are few at all levels, and competition is fierce. A vocational degree or a professional qualification (e.g. town planning, surveying, accountancy, recreation management) will help considerably. A background in journalism, public relations and designing/preparing displays is of particular use for information officer posts. Posts for **rangers** are advertised occasionally – these require a genuine interest in the countryside and outdoor activities, together with a willingness to do anything from coping with emergency rescues to posting notices and encouraging walkers to use the park facilities with care.

Theme parks and similar leisure facilities

In the commercial sector, there are a growing number of large-scale leisure attractions, incorporating things like fairground-style rides and amusements, animal collections and exhibitions of all sorts (often on a historical theme). Stately homes have gone into these sorts of ventures in a big way. Holiday centres, such as Pontins, or the newer established Center Parcs, are designed to appeal to the general public and families in particular, trying to provide 'something for everyone'. The job opportunities lie particularly in general and financial management, and marketing and promotions – obviously, some facilities need specialist staff to deal with particular themes or facilities.

The Forestry Commission

The Forestry Commission provides facilities in its many forests, including provision for activities such as orienteering, riding, and facilities for walkers, campers and picnickers. A small number of senior staff are employed on these provisions. Almost all are graduates with experience of forestry or civil engineering management, and are appointed internally.

Water companies

There are ten major water companies in England and Wales, most of which have staff in planning and/or administration, whose responsibilities include, amongst others, the recreational use of water. The personnel involved come from a wide range of backgrounds, including surveying, economics, agriculture, horticulture, landscape architecture, physical education, engineering and management.

Other opportunities

Many small organisations offer very occasional opportunities. Some of these are in the public or voluntary sectors (such as the Royal Society for the Protection of Birds), local naturalist trusts and the governing bodies of various sports. It is impossible to list all of them. A fairly comprehensive list will be found in the *Recreation Managers' Association Yearbook*, which may be available in your local library.

ENTRY AND TRAINING

There are lots of ways into careers in leisure and recreation management. A professional qualification is rarely absolutely essential, though it will be very helpful – especially if you wish to progress to more senior positions. As the number of specialist courses grows, it may well become more difficult for people without such qualifications to get started. For some types of work, specialist qualifications are needed – for instance, ability and achievement in sport. Much depends on the individual post.

There are various part-time and full-time courses which you might be interested in taking, and these lead to a wide range of qualifications. Some examples are given below, and you will be able to find others by consulting course directories.

Adults: note that maturity and previous experience may mean that stated entry requirements can be relaxed.

PART–TIME COURSES

Courses can be taken by going to college part-time, or through open learning by studying mainly at home or entirely on your own. Some of the qualifications for which you might study whilst working in relevant employment are:

- Institute of Leisure and Amenity Management qualifications;
- Institute of Sport and Recreation Management qualifications;
- City & Guilds 481 Recreation and Leisure;
- NVQ in Sport and Recreation;
- Certificate of the National Examination Board in Supervisory Management (NEBSM) in Recreation Management;
- BTEC Continuing Education Certificate in Leisure Management leading to entry to the ILAM Certificate in Leisure Management.

FULL–TIME AND SANDWICH COURSES

Consult handbooks such as the *Directory of Further Education* or the *Compendium of Higher Education* for details of courses below degree level, or use the ECCTIS database, which may be available in your local Careers Centre. Courses include Intermediate and Advanced GNVQs in Leisure and Tourism and relevant BTEC Higher National Diplomas.

There is a useful priced guide to courses produced by the Institute of Leisure and Amenity Management.

DEGREES

A degree can be a useful preparation for administrative and managerial posts in recreation/leisure provision. While job opportunities are often open to graduates from a wide range of degree subjects, it is likely that applicants who have degree subjects related to the industry may have an advantage. Relevant subjects include recreation and leisure management, sports science, sports studies and human movement studies. However, employers take a range of factors into consideration, such as experience of organising sports and social events, personal qualities and so on.

Consult the various degree course handbooks and the ECCTIS database for suitable courses. For instance, the CRAC *Degree Course Guide on Leisure and Sports Studies* is very useful.

POSTGRADUATE AND POST–EXPERIENCE COURSES

There are various diplomas and higher degrees in aspects of leisure and recreation management, intended mainly for people with some relevant work experience.

CAREERS RELATED TO SPORT

There are many ways in which you could use your interests in sport within a career. You could be directly involved in a sporting activity as a coach, for example, or work on the health, administration or management side. Entry requirements vary from few, if any, qualifications to a degree or near-equivalent.

Teaching and coaching
Teachers in schools

In state schools, specialist teachers of games, physical education, movement/dance, etc, must be qualified, like all teachers. To be a good and successful **games teacher**, you must have a real interest in teaching, as well as in sport. You will also normally need to be able to teach one other subject. Besides specialist games teachers, other secondary school teachers often help out with games teaching. All primary school teachers have scope to teach games, PE and movement to younger children. Experienced PE teachers can become teacher-trainers, or advisers on policy and standards in physical education.

QUALIFICATIONS

Basic qualifications needed to enter a teacher training course (Bachelor of Education degree) are two A levels (or the equivalent) plus supporting GCSEs which must include mathematics and English. If you are exceptionally talented at sport you might be allowed, at the discretion of individual colleges, to enter training with only one A level.

It is not essential to be qualified to teach in an independent school (though many teachers are fully trained, and individual schools set their own requirements). Sport is given a high priority in many independent schools, and there are very good opportunities. There is more specialisation (e.g. teacher in charge of cricket, rugby, hockey, etc) and more work in running teams and organising matches. In these schools, it is very common for younger teachers of other subjects to help out with games lessons, practices, etc.

Larger independent schools may employ **professional coaches** who are not teachers but experts in their sport.

See the later section on teaching sport and PE for further information.

Sports and exercise coaches and instructors

Coaches and **instructors** are usually concerned with just one particular sport – such as tennis, skiing, judo, swimming, trampolining. They may work with young people and children in schools, in sports centres used by schools, and youth clubs. They can also instruct adults, through evening classes, sports clubs, university and college sports centres, etc. There are also opportunities to work with people undertaking physical activity as part of their work training – for example in jobs where self-defence is taught. For some sports, there are opportunities in private clubs – particularly for golf professionals, tennis and squash coaches, sailing instructors, instructors in the martial arts, and swimming coaches. This can involve instructing children and adults.

One area which has grown in recent years is that of keep-fit and aerobics. Various courses (many of them part-time) are available to train instructors. Some are offered through colleges of further education, others by private organisations and well-known exercise studios. It is important to ensure that any course you take will be acceptable to prospective employers.

Instructing and coaching may be just a part-time job, though large centres employ **full-time instructors** if there is enough demand. Others may build up enough part-time instruction to make up a full-time work load. The governing bodies of most sports offer their own instructor qualifications, and these are usually required if you want to instruct for payment. Most people study for these qualifications in their leisure time. The National Coaching Foundation offers courses which complement these qualifications, from introductory to advanced level.

There are also opportunities for teachers, qualified outdoor pursuits instructors and sports enthusiasts to work for companies running children's and adults' activity holidays, holiday camps, on board ship, or within the recreational programmes of colleges which offer English language tuition for foreign students, etc. These jobs are often seasonal only. The Central Council of Physical Recreation runs a Community Sports Leaders Award Scheme, which may be a suitable starting point.

Another employment area is within the Armed Forces, which have physical education instructors of a very high standard – enquire at your nearest Armed Forces Careers Information Office.

Management and administrative work

This sort of work does not normally involve physical activity (though there may be some opportunity for instructing, etc), but it is done in a sporting context. It covers work like sports centre management, swimming pool, gymnasium and health club management, the organisation of sporting events, and some administrative posts with sporting organisations such as the Sports Council and the governing bodies of various individual sports. Certainly an enthusiasm for sport is a big asset, and will help in promoting the organisation for which you work; however, it is not usually essential to be a competent sports person.

To do this sort of work, you may need a degree or diploma in a subject related to sports/recreation management. Previous administrative experience or business training is very helpful. There are also posts for secretaries and all the other office staff which any organisation needs to keep things running.

Sports equipment and clothing manufacturers also need administrators, as well as people to work in areas like public relations, marketing and selling, where a knowledge of, and interest in, sport is important. Retailing sports equipment and clothing is another area of opportunity, with a number of multiple retailers having appeared in recent years, to satisfy the growing need for sportswear and equipment.

Health and medical opportunities

Sports medicine and physiology

The study of the physiological aspects of sport is a postgraduate specialism taken up by a small number of qualified doctors, physiologists and related scientists. Besides opportunities in research, some practitioners act as consultants to national teams, etc. There are also teaching and lecturing posts – for example in colleges where sports science is taught.

Physiotherapy and sports therapy

Physiotherapists and other similar practitioners are employed to advise and treat sportsmen and women – you've probably seen the football club's 'physio' rush on to the pitch during a match to look at an injured player. Treatment may include massage, electrical, heat and hydrotherapy to restore injured limbs to full working order. They may also advise on exercise routines, proper use of the body in training, and so on.

This type of work is done by **chartered physiotherapists** (a long-standing profession), **masseurs**, and by people with newer titles such as **sports therapists**. Qualifying as a chartered physiotherapist is likely to give you the most employment opportunities, including many outside sport. However, the alternative qualifications available appear to be in reasonable demand in what is a growth area.

Some physiotherapists work in private practice and deal with amateur and professional sportspeople as their speciality, though probably alongside patients who have no connection with sport. Others work for health clubs and gymnasiums, dealing mainly with people participating in sport as a leisure activity.

See the section on physiotherapy and sports therapy for further information.

Other ways of using an interest in sport

Lifeguards and swimming pool attendants – you need to hold either the National Beach Lifeguard or National Pool Lifeguard qualification (NVQ level 2) offered by the Royal Life-Saving Society. The smaller Surf Life-Saving Association also offers a beach lifeguard qualification.

Greenkeeping and grounds staff – this involves managing the turf (natural and synthetic) of sports facilities and surrounding areas: see *Horticulture, Forestry & Farming* in the *Just the Job!* series.

Sports journalists and photographers – there are two main routes in to this work: either by starting as an ordinary journalist or after experience as a sports 'personality' of some kind. Photographers and TV camera operators would need to do normal training. Some freelance work for both reporters and photographers is available, particularly with local papers.

Jobs where sport is particularly encouraged, or where sports facilities are especially good – this includes jobs where you are expected to maintain a high degree of fitness, such as the Armed Forces, police, fire service, etc. Some large organisations, such as banks, are noted for their good staff sports facilities, especially in larger cities.

Keeping sport as a hobby

Of course, if none of these job ideas is a realistic idea for you, you can always keep up your interest in sport in your leisure time. This is possible whatever sort of work you do, or even if you do not have paid employment. A leisure interest which you really enjoy can often make up for a boring or unpleasant job.

Adults: note that, for many of the jobs mentioned here, younger people may be preferred because of the amount of physical activity involved. For jobs in which your age would not be a disadvantage, you should note that educational requirements may be relaxed in view of maturity and experience.

SPORT & RELATED SUBJECTS AT HIGHER EDUCATION LEVEL

At higher education level, there are many degree and diploma courses in physical education, sports science, sports studies, human movement studies, etc. While each course is different, they all involve the study of people both as individuals and as members of groups in the context of sports, games and dance.

Degrees in sport and related subjects are offered by universities and colleges of higher education. Courses can be single subject ordinary or honours degrees, joint degrees, or combined studies degrees which allow students to follow several subjects. Some institutions also offer BTEC Higher National Diploma and Diploma of Higher Education courses. Degree, HND and Dip HE courses all attract mandatory awards, so you can apply to whichever university or college you wish.

There is also a range of postgraduate courses, including the Postgraduate Certificate in Education (PGCE) for prospective teachers, which specialise in aspects of physical education or sports science, management, therapy, etc.

Course content

You must read the university and college prospectuses carefully in order to choose the most appropriate course. Amongst topics offered are biology of physical activity, exercise physiology, biomechanics, psychology of sport, leisure management, social and historical aspects of sport and games, comparative studies and the study and practice of sporting skills. Some of the sports science courses need a strong science background, while others have more of an orientation towards social sciences.

Degree programmes in movement studies often have a common foundation year, followed by an opportunity to specialise in areas which could lead to careers in education, leisure or sports science. There are also options covering the performing arts, involving study of dance, drama and music.

The practical content of each course varies considerably, and the emphasis placed on sporting ability as part of the selection procedure varies from institution to institution. Some seek candidates of county standard in their main sport, while others merely look for 'strong interest'.

ENTRY QUALIFICATIONS

For a degree or Dip HE course, at least two A levels are normally needed, plus supporting GCSEs. Equivalent qualifications such as a BTEC National Diploma or an Advanced GNVQ may well be accepted: check with individual institutions. A very small percentage of places may be offered at some colleges to candidates with only one A level, whose sporting performance and experience (e.g. national representation) may be accepted as an alternative. The subjects required at A level vary, but a science A level is required or preferred for a significant number of courses. Intending teachers in state schools should note that mathematics and English at GCSE grade C or above (or equivalent) are essential, whether you train to teach through a BEd or postgraduate course. Entry requirements for BTEC HND are normally one A level plus three or four GCSEs at C or above, or a high standard in a BTEC National Diploma or Certificate.

CAREER PROSPECTS

In recent years, there has been a considerable increase in leisure and recreation activities, both as private ventures and through local authorities. Graduates from sports-related courses seem to be successful in finding relevant employment.

Some of the employment areas which graduates have entered in the past are: in education as teachers, lecturers and administrators; in recreation management – leisure centres, sports centres, etc; coaching, and exercise clinics; equipment firms; the Armed Forces and police; research; and the media and journalism. Some graduates use their degree as a sign of general ability and take up work with no particular relevance to physical education. Some with joint degrees may make use of their other main subject in a career, or, if they are lucky, find an opportunity which combines both areas of study.

PROFESSIONAL SPORT

For a career in professional sport, you have to be very talented! In most sports, you will know by school-leaving age whether or not you have a genuine talent. Are you playing for your school first team, county or regional team? Do you belong to a club and regularly come top in your age group? If your answer to these questions is 'no', then professional sport is probably not for you.

There are other considerations besides talent. Professional sport is a hard life. Are you prepared to train and train? Accept low wages with a chance of great things later? Take the risks of a job where an injury could wreck your career before it has started? Do you want a career where you could be finished at the age of 25 or 30?

A look at football shows what can happen. Some football clubs sign on young hopefuls, then two years later say 'no thank you', leaving the young player to rethink their career. This happens to 75% of footballers by the age of 21. Professional sport isn't just cup finals. It's also playing for a fourth-division reserve team on a freezing, foggy January afternoon – or even not being selected to play for the reserves!

A second career

All professional sportspeople need a second career. This might involve something to take up when their sporting life is over, or perhaps to follow out of the sporting season. Or it might be a

THEN THE SATELLITE CHANNELS GOT INTERESTED IN TIDDLEY WINKS AND THE REST IS HISTORY

THE WINKA!

job which will earn them a living while they try to make a go of a sports career in, say, darts, athletics or boxing. What they do might be quite unrelated to sport.

Many ex-sports professionals now run pubs and shops, for instance, using money put aside in their sporting career to set themselves up. The main thing is not to cut yourself off from any other reasonable career opportunities that might be open to you. Take your education as far as you can. There are graduate footballers, cricketers and tennis players around. GCSEs, A levels, Advanced GNVQ, FE college courses, Open University – everything helps.

Sports with opportunities for professionals

Sports where professional players can earn a living are few. Also, there are fewer opportunities for women than for men.

In this country, the main sports offering opportunities for professionals include basketball, boxing, cricket, cycling, darts, football, golf, horse-racing, motorcycling, motor-racing, rugby, snooker and tennis. In some of these sports, such as motor-racing or cycling, the numbers of professionals are very few, whilst even in the sports employing higher numbers of professionals, such as football, competition is intense. There are also some opportunities for professionals in showjumping, skiing and skating. British athletics has effectively become professional, with top athletes getting large payments in the form of sponsorships and appearance money. Of course, many sports are international. Sportspeople can compete abroad or play for foreign teams, and there are greater opportunities overseas in some sports. Each sport has a governing body which can advise on opportunities. The Sports Council (see Further Information section) will provide addresses.

Emma – golf professional

I was always good at sports at school, but I didn't discover golf until my uncle treated me to a lesson for my 18th birthday. I didn't really expect to like it much, but got instantly hooked. By that time, I was able to kit myself out at discount!

Once I'd got my handicap down to a decent level, I pestered all the professionals at local golf clubs until one of them took me on as a probationer. I passed the Professional Golfers' Association exam in English and Maths (as I didn't have grade C at GCSE). After six months I was able to register as a PGA trainee. Training was mostly at my club, but also on a couple of residential courses. A trainee is a bit of a dogsbody, helping the club professional in cleaning premises and equipment, working in the shop and so on. In the meantime, you learn how to teach, how to run the business side of a club, golf rules and regulations and tournament organisation. All the while you're improving your own game.

I passed the PGA final exams after four years, so I'm now qualified, but still working for my original boss. Eventually, I hope to set myself up as professional in another club. This takes quite a lot of money, as you have to stock the shop yourself. I was surprised at first to find out how important the commercial side of being a professional is, but it's quite interesting when you get used to it. I'm now playing in some of the smaller tournaments. I don't think I'll ever be a top player, but at least I'm working at something I really enjoy doing.

EMPLOYER–BASED TRAINING IN PROFESSIONAL SPORT

Employer-based training is available to young people interested in a career in various sports, often leading to National Vocational Qualifications.

Football
The Footballers' Further Education and Vocational Training Society Ltd (see Further Information section) provides school-leavers not just with first-class training in football, but also with

planned work experience and general education, so that the many boys who do not eventually become professionals will have other skills which they can use.

Other sports

There are also some training opportunities in snooker, as trainee golf professionals, and in cricket, sailing, and ice-skating and possibly other sports. In many sports, it is necessary to do extremely well as an amateur before even thinking about turning professional.

Contact your local careers service for information and advice, and keep in touch with the governing body of your chosen sport.

Non-playing jobs in sport

Many sports enthusiasts get great pleasure from their game as an amateur, without the stress and risk of the professional life. But if you don't make the grade as a professional, there other sports-related jobs which you can think about.

TEACHING SPORT & PE

Teachers of physical education work mostly in secondary schools, teaching games, gymnastics, dance, athletics, swimming and outdoor activities, such as canoeing and rock climbing – the range varies between individual schools. They also organise matches and help with extracurricular clubs. Teaching is virtually an all-graduate profession for new entrants.

Physical education in schools is concerned both with encouraging pupils' skills and body management and with young people's healthy growth and development. It is also a useful preparation for the management of leisure as adults.

Commonly, PE specialists teach another subject – this could be any one of the curriculum options, but it is useful to offer a mainstream subject. Of course, all primary school teachers have the scope to teach PE, games and movement to younger children, but this section concentrates on teaching PE as a specialist subject.

What the work involves

PE teachers need to like and understand children and teenagers, and need to want to help them develop. A friendly but firm manner, patience, energy and organising skills are required. Fitness and skill in sport and movement are also very important. You are likely to spend a lot of time in out-of-school activities. After-school and Saturday matches, practices and clubs are all part of the job, besides the usual marking and lesson preparation, duties of a form teacher, etc. You may be responsible for pupils studying PE up to GCSE and A level standard.

Both state and independent schools can place a very high emphasis on PE, sport and team games, and specialist posts are frequently advertised. Managing teams is an important part of the work, with a considerable commitment to midweek and weekend matches. Whilst there is no legal requirement for teachers in independent schools to have had formal teacher training (as there is in state schools), many independent schools insist on teachers being qualified and capable of teaching an additional subject.

TRAINING TO TEACH

Teaching is now, for new entrants, generally an all-graduate profession, so you must have a degree, and there are two main routes:

- The Bachelor of Education (BEd), gained through a three-year or four-year degree course, is the more popular entry route for primary teachers. Several institutions offer BEd degrees with PE options at secondary level.
- Most secondary teachers take a BA or BSc first degree in the subject they wish to teach, followed by a postgraduate certificate in education (PGCE). The first degree must be appropriate to the curricular work in schools and colleges.

Specialist training for graduates wishing to teach PE is available in a number of universities and colleges. Some of these courses may be taken after any degree, although some institutions prefer students who have taken PE, sports science or human movement as at least a major part of their undergraduate course. There is also evidence that employment prospects are better for students who have taken one of these subjects as their first degree. A limited number of one-year postgraduate courses are provided through school-centred initial teacher training courses.

School/college-leavers: to get on to a degree course as a school/college-leaver normally requires a minimum of two A levels (or the equivalent) plus supporting GCSEs. Some PE and dance applicants may be accepted on to a BEd course with one A level, if they offer an extremely high standard in their practical subject.

Adults with few or no qualifications wanting to train for teaching could follow an Access course. These courses are offered at many further education colleges and are designed as an alternative to GCSEs and A levels for entry to degree and other higher education courses (minimum age varies between 21 and 24 years). For PE teaching, clearly a high level of physical fitness is demanded, and mature applicants need to be aware that their career opportunities could be very limited.

Note: all applicants for teacher training are required to have GCSE at grade C or above in both English language and mathematics (or equivalent qualifications). Some colleges allow applicants over 25 to take an entrance test if they have had no opportunity to gain such exam passes. For students born on or after 1 September 1979, a GCSE in a science subject (grade A–C) is required for entry to primary teacher training from September 1998.

The Licensed Teacher Scheme operates in some parts of the country. This allows unqualified people to enter teaching and gain their training on-the-job, over two years. Applicants must be aged 24 or over, and need to have studied successfully for at least two years at higher education level. Realistically, opportunities for entering PE teaching this way are likely to be very limited, because of the age of applicants. Contact the Teacher Training Agency (see Further Information section) for details.

PROSPECTS

On the whole, people with a relevant degree plus a PGCE qualification from a university seem to have least difficulty in finding employment. Being able to offer a second teaching subject that is in demand will improve your chances of getting a job. You should also think ahead to when you are older – as the physical aspects of the job become less attractive and more arduous, an alternative teaching subject will almost certainly be required. The areas where there is most demand for teachers at present are in the 'shortage' subjects of sciences, mathematics, modern languages and design technology.

Other openings

Sports coaching at sport and leisure centres does not demand such high academic qualifications, but you will be expected to have appropriate practical qualifications in your chosen sport or sports.

PHYSIOTHERAPY & SPORTS THERAPY

Physiotherapy and sports therapy are career areas concerned with human movement and exercise. Nowadays,
many people are interested in health and fitness, and this has
been reflected in a mushrooming of sports and leisure clubs
around the country. Opportunities in this field are growing
steadily for those with recognised qualifications, which can
range from a certificate to a specialised degree.

If you want to work in physiotherapy within the National
Health Service, you need to become a **chartered physiotherapist**, as this is the only qualification which makes you eligible
for state registration, a statutory requirement for health service
work. Qualifying as a chartered physiotherapist opens a number
of career possibilities to you. About 85% of chartered physiotherapists are female, though the proportion of male practitioners is growing rapidly. British qualifications are generally
accepted abroad and employment prospects, both at home and
abroad, are good.

Physiotherapists in the health service

Most physiotherapists are based in the physiotherapy departments of general hospitals, but, in fact, work in many different
departments. For instance, they can work in medical and surgical wards, burns units and intensive care units. Some work in
rehabilitation centres and often visit patients in their own
homes. Increasingly, physiotherapists work in the community,
either in community units or attached to GPs' surgeries.

What do physiotherapists do?

Physiotherapists work as part of a team with doctors, nurses, social workers, radiographers and occupational therapists. They do, however, make their own diagnoses and devise courses of treatment.

Physiotherapists deal with problems concerned with loss of movement resulting from illness, injury or the onset of old age. Due to loss of movement, patients may be unable to wash and dress themselves, look after the house or go to work. Physiotherapists assist these people to regain their independence. They may also devise programmes for the healthy in order to avoid problems developing. Besides illness and injury cases, physiotherapists also help permanently disabled people to develop their full potential.

Physiotherapy work programmes

Physiotherapists must have a sound knowledge of how a healthy body works in normal movement, and the factors which can impair this, in order to employ their techniques of manipulation and massage. To this end, they study in great detail the structure and function of bones, muscles, joints and nerves.

Work with a patient often starts immediately after an operation. The physiotherapist formulates a treatment programme by comparing the weaknesses and deficiencies in the patient with normal movements. Treatment must be decided upon and put into effect. The programme may involve using heat or ice to relieve pain, or electrical currents which will make weak muscles contract and show the patient how to use them again. Even more important is teaching patients exercises which will loosen stiff joints, strengthen weak muscles and coordinate their movements.

CAREER DEVELOPMENT

Experienced physiotherapists can specialise in geriatric work, or work in orthopaedic or chest hospitals, with children in their own homes, or in hospitals or schools for children with disabilities. They do not necessarily work just with sick and injured people. They also work with expectant and newly delivered mothers in antenatal clinics and maternity hospitals, teaching relaxation, breathing and muscle-strengthening exercises. There are various post-qualifying courses which can be taken in specialist areas of work. It is also possible to become a teacher of physiotherapy, once qualified and with experience.

Opportunities outside the health service

Many physiotherapists leave NHS work to run their own private practices, or perhaps do some private work in addition to their health service work. Sports clubs, health farms, etc, employ physiotherapists to keep their members fit and treat injuries, though practitioners other than chartered physiothera-pists are also employed to do this sort of work. Industrial organ-isations may employ physiotherapists for preventive work, such as training porters to carry without strain, or teaching sales assis-tants to relax while standing.

QUALIFICATIONS AND TRAINING

There is a lot of competition for training places, with about ten applicants per place.

To qualify as a **chartered physiotherapist**, you first have to complete a three- or four-year degree course in physiotherapy.

Most schools of physiotherapy are based in higher education institutions, while others are attached to hospitals and are recog-nised by the Chartered Society of Physiotherapy. Applicants are advised to contact individual institutions for their entry require-ments.

The training syllabus covers:

- physiology, anatomy, behavioural science, physics, theory and practice of movement, electrotherapy and manipulative procedures;
- the medical and surgical conditions for which physiotherapy may be used;
- handling patients (psychologically, as well as physically).

For the first few months, training is entirely theoretical, but, from then on, it is a combination of theory and practice. This includes regular work with patients in physiotherapy depart-ments and on the wards, under the supervision of trained physiotherapists.

What it takes
Age and physique
The minimum age for training is 18 and the usual maximum is 35. You need to be physically fit. However, some disabilities are acceptable. Prospective students with a visual impairment should discuss training opportunities with the RNIB Physiotherapy Support Service (see Further Information section).

Educational requirements
Candidates usually need at least five GCSEs at grade C and three A levels, or an Advanced GNVQ/BTEC National Diploma. Additional units, or a science A level, may be required as well as an Advanced GNVQ. An access course in science is appropriate for mature students. GCSEs must include English language, maths and science (including some physics). One of the A levels should preferably be biology (at grade C or better). Successful applicants usually have at least three grade Cs at A level.

Personality
Besides academic qualifications, the ability to communicate is regarded as very important, as is warmth of manner, commonsense, humour, tolerance and patience. These qualities are necessary to establish good relations with patients.

GETTING STARTED

It is very important that prospective students have visited a physiotherapy department, so that they have some awareness of what is involved. Applications to physiotherapy courses are made through UCAS – applicants are recommended to choose only four; the remaining choices may be used for alternative courses such as physiology or biology. The Chartered Society produces a free leaflet which explains the application procedure for individual physiotherapy courses (see Further Information section for address).

Mature students

Physiotherapy is a profession which welcomes the older student. About one-third of all UK students are over 21 when they begin training. A mature student thinking of applying for physiotherapy needs to show evidence of having given their decision serious thought. This could be achieved through visiting local physiotherapy departments, attending any available open days and, if possible, obtaining relevant work and voluntary experience as, for example, a physiotherapy helper, assistant in a sport injury clinic or a school for children with disabilities.

As mentioned above, access courses in science are a possible entry route for adults without the usual academic qualifications. There are a few access courses specifically linked to physiotherapy degree courses.

Physiotherapy courses demand the ability to study and to apply sound scientific and professional knowledge to problem-solving. Before you can be accepted onto a course, you will need to show evidence of recent academic application. It is often advisable to study A level biology or human biology for a year at evening class, for example. If you have already gained higher-level qualifications in another field, you need to check your eligibility for a grant, which will depend on the type of course for which you may already have had financial assistance.

Physiotherapy aide/helper

In the health service, **physiotherapy aides** help qualified physiotherapists in hospital physiotherapy departments. It's a job which offers a lot of contact with patients, without the high-level qualifications needed to become a chartered physiotherapist. The helpers look after patients who are having treatment, assisting them to undress and dress if necessary. They help to set up apparatus and tidy it away after use, and, under the super-vision of a physiotherapist, help patients with exercises. Training is generally on-the-job.

You don't need any special educational qualifications to do this work, but you need to be fit and active, reliable, and good with people. As with most medically related work, it's no good being squeamish.

Maturity is an advantage, and so is experience in related work – as a care assistant, for example.

Sports therapist

The term *sports therapist* has become familiar in recent years, arising out of the expansion of sports, health and leisure facili-ties. Both local authority-owned facilities and private exercise clubs have increased considerably in number, creating a demand for suitably qualified people not only to run them, but also to ensure that the equipment is used properly and that users under-take exercise suitable to their level of fitness.

The work of sports therapists covers many activities. They use various massage techniques, saunas, hydrotherapy baths and electronic muscle exercisers. There is also keep-fit and dance exercise, and the use of gymnasium and sophisticated exercise equipment.

On the whole, sports therapists work with people who are basi-cally well, but who wish to improve their level of fitness, or who have minor sports injuries. Besides health and fitness clubs, exer-cise classes, etc, they might work for professional sports clubs and may build up a career through a collection of part-time commit-ments. Some sports therapy practitioners may specialise in just one aspect of the work, while others will have qualifications in a range of skills and techniques. Obviously, the wider the range of qualifications offered, the better the choice of jobs will be.

Some sports therapists work as personal trainers, giving individual attention to a small number of people, helping them to maintain their overall health and fitness, often within a busy social and business schedule.

Zak – physiotherapist in a health club

' I've always enjoyed a challenge, so when I discovered that the profession I wanted to enter was dominated by women, I wasn't daunted! In fact, more men are becoming physios now anyway. It's not easy to get started: I needed three good A levels, including a science. Then the hard work really began – three years of study to qualify, then six years working in a hospital before I landed this job.

In the hospital you deal with a variety of patients, many of them over a long period of time. Here, at the health club, I get to see people for shorter periods of time, as they've usually come for a few weeks to recuperate from an illness or injury, or they get injured at the club and need help before coming home. I use all kinds of exercises and movement to get people mobile again. People generally prefer it when I massage them to when I manipulate their limbs, but they don't get the choice! There's a lovely warm swimming pool here, and I often use the heat of the water as a source of treatment. '

QUALIFICATIONS AND TRAINING

People at present employed in sports therapy have a variety of backgrounds and qualifications, perhaps physiotherapy or remedial gymnastics, or an alternative medical practice such as osteopathy or chiropractic. Some have sports science degrees, a PE/movement teaching qualification, experience as a PE instructor in the Forces, or one of the many qualifications available in keep-fit/exercise instruction or massage. Each offers certain advantages and it is not really possible to say categorically which might be the 'best' background.

In addition, the International Institute of Sports Therapy (IIST) provides specific sports therapy syllabuses and qualifications. Because these qualifications are based on assessment of skills and competencies, there are no rigid age or educational requirements for entry. Entry requirements to courses are at the discretion of individual colleges, who may be particularly lenient with mature applicants.

Fitness and Sports Therapy Assistant Certificate – a basic qualification for helpers in health and fitness clubs, etc.

Sports Massage Certificate – covers massage and remedial exercises.

International Fitness and Sports Therapy Diploma – covers massage, remedial exercises, operation and maintenance of sauna equipment, steam baths, gymnasium equipment, ultraviolet and infra-red lamps, plus techniques for testing physical function and applying corrective treatment apparatus, such as electronic muscle exercisers and vacuum suction units.

International Master's Diploma in Sports Therapy – all the subject matter of the Fitness and Sports Therapy Diploma plus more extensive knowledge of anatomy and physiology, fitness, body alignment and evaluation of test procedures; you have to write a thesis on a research topic.

International Teacher's Diploma in Sports Therapy – available only to those with the IIST Master's Diploma, Fitness and Sports Therapy Diploma, or equivalent.

Courses for these qualifications are offered at only a few further education colleges, but these are growing in number, so check with the Institute.

CAREERS IN OUTDOOR PURSUITS

The term *outdoor pursuits* includes a wide range of activities – such as climbing, orienteering, riding, sailing, windsurfing and canoeing, even parachuting and hang-gliding. It also covers different types of employment within the fields of leisure and education. Qualifications in your chosen activity can be as important as academic qualifications for some jobs, while others may require a degree.

Teaching in schools

There are few opportunities for people to be employed in schools, whether state or private, specifically as teachers of outdoor pursuits. It is usual to teach another subject too. However, outdoor pursuits can be taken as a special option on some teacher training courses. There are also specialist BEd and postgraduate degree courses in outdoor education. See the *Handbook of Initial Teacher Training*, published by NATFHE, for details of all BEd and PGCE courses.

Teachers with such qualifications, or simply with an interest in one or more types of activity, may well be able to find some opportunities for developing children's interest in outdoor pursuits, but this might be outside normal school work – for instance, through after-school clubs, the Duke of Edinburgh's Award Scheme or taking occasional parties of children to outdoor activity centres.

Teaching & instructing in outdoor activity centres

Many local education authorities maintain outdoor activity/education centres, to which schools send parties of children for a few days or a week at a time. These centres require well-trained and experienced **outdoor pursuits staff**. Some would want qualified teachers, others would accept instructors trained in individual activities such as canoeing and mountaineering. Few job vacancies occur, however, and huge numbers apply for those that do. There are also opportunities in privately run centres, and places such as artificial ski slopes. Appropriate instructor qualifications are essential. Outward Bound Centres also employ instructors/tutors – though, again, few posts occur. Qualified instructors could also seek work abroad.

Youth work

It is certainly an asset for youth workers and others involved in young people's leisure activities to be keen on outdoor pursuits. Both full-time professional youth workers, and those who are youth leaders, Scouters, Guiders, etc, in their spare time, can use an interest in such activities. But it's only incidental to the work: organisational abilities and a genuine interest in young people are a much greater priority.

Adventure holidays, etc

There are quite a lot of private holiday companies and centres which offer 'activity' or 'adventure' holidays for unaccompanied children, family groups, and adults. Outdoor pursuits often feature amongst the activities on offer – for example sailing, canoeing, orienteering. Employment is often seasonal, with teachers and students being taken on for summer work. Instructor and/or teaching qualifications are a great asset.

QUALIFICATIONS

Each activity, such as canoeing or horseriding, has its own controlling body which trains instructors. A useful initial qualification is the Central Council of Physical Recreation's Basic Expedition Training Award.

Other opportunities

People with very high-level qualifications in a particular activity could become trainers. Experienced people can run weekend/short courses, either in the skills of a particular activity, or to train people to become coaches or instructors. Very limited openings exist in specialised areas such as the provision of activities for disabled youngsters and adults. There are opportunities within the Armed Forces, not only for instructors, but for all recruits – as sport, outdoor activities and physical education play a very important part in the training of all Forces personnel. You can also accumulate a wide range of coaching qualifications if you wish. The Police Force also offers good opportunities.

DIVING

Diving as a job sounds exciting and not really like work at all. But the reality is not so simple. As a commercial diver, you must have an HSE (Health & Safety Executive) certificate of diver training, a certificate of diving first aid and a current certificate of medical fitness in order to carry out your work.

Although it can be very interesting to work underwater, professional diving can be hazardous and exhausting – even extremely boring at times. **Deep-sea divers** spend a lot of time just sitting around in a decompression chamber waiting for their bodies to readjust to surface conditions.

Air diving

Down to depths of 50 metres, divers can breathe compressed air, either from cylinders carried on their backs, or through hoses from the surface. For the basic air diving course you must be a good swimmer, physically fit, and hold a valid certificate of medical fitness to dive. This certificate has to be renewed annually by an HSE-approved doctor. Diving experience is not essential. Training lasts several weeks and fees can run to thousands of pounds. Employer sponsorship is not available.

Mixed-gas diving

Below 50 metres, divers must breathe a mixture of oxygen with helium, or another inert gas. *Saturation diving* is the main technique used. Divers, whose blood is saturated with the inert gas, live in a compression chamber for as much as a month at a time, being transported to and from the seabed in a pressurised diving bell. Very strict routines and discipline are essential to avoid accidents. For the mixed-gas diving course, you must be a competent and qualified **air diver** with a year's experience of working down to 50 metres, and have a current certificate of medical fitness to dive from an HSE-approved doctor.

Diving – the facts

- Diving is a means of transportation to a place where a job needs doing, whether it is maintaining an oil rig, photographing an underwater structure or recovering a body.
- Divers wear heavy suits, breathing apparatus and possibly have additional hoses connecting them to their life-support system.
- To work as a diver in the UK you need an HSE certificate of diver training to prove that you have completed an HSE-approved course of instruction at a diving school.
- Inshore diving includes marine civil engineering (port and harbour construction and repair), salvage, archaeology, film-making, forecasting of underwater conditions, scientific research and fish farming.
- Offshore diving can involve working anywhere in the world. Work is contract-based and can be seasonal. Most offshore work in the UK is in the North Sea oil and gas industries, where divers are employed to carry out inspections, and construction, maintenance or demolition work.
- Inspection of an underwater structure may involve examining it by eye, taking photographs and using an underwater TV camera.
- Construction and demolition work could involve thermal cutting, welding, placing explosives, using power tools and cementing.
- Pay can be good for experienced divers.
- It's a short working life – few people over 45 continue diving offshore.

GETTING STARTED

You don't need any particular educational qualifications, but GCSEs at grade C in maths and English, or equivalent qualifications, are useful. Engineering, construction or scientific skills will help when seeking employment as a commercial diver. At the present time, it is difficult for the trained, but inexperienced, diver to find employment in the commercial diving field.

Remember:

- Diving is very demanding, both physically and mentally, so excellent health is essential. There are thorough annual medical checks.
- Many would-be divers drop out because they cannot cope with the tough training. Diving does require a special form of courage.

Training courses are currently offered at five approved centres (see Further Information section). Career development loans may be available to meet the cost of training as a commercial diver. Ask for details at your local Jobcentre.

The offshore diving industry

International diving contracting companies operate worldwide in the oil and gas industries. They employ **offshore divers**, usually on short contracts of a few months. Willingness to travel worldwide is vital and is normally at the diver's own expense! The unsettled nature of the work can be hard to combine with family life.

Other opportunities

- **Police** divers are employed in specialist diving units.
- **Army** divers are part of Royal Engineer units employed mainly on underwater construction and engineering tasks.

- **Royal Navy** divers work on underwater ship repair, salvage operations, demolition and explosives disposal.
- **Royal Marine** divers specialise in underwater military operations.

Note: The Armed Forces or police give no guarantees of being chosen for diving training. Trainees are selected from personnel already in service.

- There is limited inshore air and scuba diving employment for **marine biologists**, **archaeologists** and **photographers/ camera operators**. You need outstanding specialist knowledge to make a career in these areas.
- Working as a **diving instructor** in either commercial or sports diving training is a possibility for the well-qualified and experienced diver.
- **Life-support technicians** look after divers in decompression chambers.

just
THE
JOB

ENTERTAINING & SHOW BUSINESS

> *Entertainer* is a term used to describe a wide range of performers: comedians, cabaret singers, musicians, dancers, puppeteers, conjurors, mime artists, jugglers, acrobats, impressionists – even animal trainers. There are also host/hostess-entertainers, who organise and entertain their audiences in places like holiday centres, large hotels and on board cruise ships.

Where do entertainers work?

- Television offers opportunities for top-grade entertainers, but it's very hard to break in.
- Theatres put on pantomimes in the winter and summer shows at seaside resorts.
- Social clubs and a number of pubs employ entertainers of all kinds, but mainly comedians and singers, and this is where many people gain experience and build up their reputations.
- Exclusive nightclubs usually employ top-class entertainers.
- Holiday camps/centres and theme parks offer opportunities for people to organise social events and entertain as well. This work is a training ground for many hopeful entertainers.
- Cruise ships employ staff to organise general passenger entertainment.
- Circuses employ certain specialist entertainers.
- Other opportunities include entertaining at events like children's parties and medieval banquets.

■ Street entertainers can operate under licence from local authorities and police in shopping precincts or town centres, or as part of festivals and carnivals.

GETTING STARTED

Obviously, the first thing is to decide where your talents lie, and whether you really have the drive to make it in the entertainment business. Probably you will spend a long time as an amateur or part-time entertainer, doing evening and weekend performances, whilst having an ordinary daytime job, before you consider going professional.

However, at a fairly early stage, you are likely to need an agent to get bookings for you. You'll have to convince them that you have an act that people will want, and that you are 100% reliable. There are many agents in London and other city centres who book for clubs and events like conventions, conferences, dances and so forth.

Things to think about . . .

- Being an entertainer is an odd, stressful and chancy business. There are many people around in show business who, if not exactly dishonest, are quite prepared to make money out of the unwary and inexperienced.
- Nobody gets to the top without some knocks, and most never get to the top anyway. You'll need a lot of perseverance and some good luck.
- The lifestyle may be difficult. The hours are unsocial, as you are working when most people are at leisure. It can be stressful working in different places all the time, sometimes with hostile audiences.
- Regular work is unusual, so earnings can be very irregular too. You will certainly need an alternative way of making your living, if necessary.

Entertaining can be an *international* business, though that does depend on your act. Obviously, comedians can only work with audiences who understand their language (and, usually, culture).

If you are a conjuror or a dancer, however, you could look for work further afield.

Cruise ships employ an entertainments officer or cruise director or social host/hostess: the actual duties and levels of responsibility may vary with the job title. Work involves playing host to passengers and organising passenger entertainments. Relevant experience and being able to sing, dance or entertain in some way would be expected. A lively personality and stamina are other essential requirements.

There is usually plenty of free time to use the facilities on board – cinema, bars and gym – and also to go onshore.

Holiday camps/centres and **theme parks** employ entertainers to organise daily activities for holiday-makers, to socialise with guests and participate in entertainments. Much work is involved in keeping children safely entertained! This type of entertainment work may only be seasonal.

CAREERS FOR MUSICIANS

'Music' covers a very wide range of activities – from pop to opera, and from playing the rackett (a kind of squashed-up medieval bassoon) to the synthesiser. In this section, you can find out about the different careers for musicians which involve you in going to music college or perhaps taking a music degree.

Performing

You have to be exceptionally talented to make a career as a performer in any field. In the world of classical music, only about 2000 musicians can get full-time work in British orchestras, and very few openings come up each year. Solo performers find it even harder to make a living – far fewer of them are needed.

Most performers are drawn from students from the colleges of music. Students who have studied for a music degree usually take a postgraduate course at one of the music colleges, in order to concentrate on technique and repertoire, since, on the whole, university courses do not have a strong performance bias. Those who have taken a performance course at a music department may be better prepared than those who have taken a purely academic course, but, even so, a music college is valuable for building contacts. Most performers accept a mixture of solo, choral/orchestral and ensemble engagements to start with, although **instrumentalists** may join full-time professional orchestras.

When they get very busy, **soloists** generally employ an agent to arrange their engagements. The BBC gives radio auditions to experienced soloists. Recording companies, schools and other organisations employ accompanists, who are good at sight-reading and improvisation, and répétiteurs or coaches. **Organists** may find employment in churches and cathedrals and, occasionally, in university colleges and public schools (where teaching is often required as well).

GETTING STARTED

If you want a performing career as a **pop artist** or **dance band musician**, you need to be talented, and a proficient instrumentalist or singer, if you're going to get anywhere. Although a college training is not essential, there are some degree and BTEC HND courses available in popular music. The City of Leeds College of Music offers a degree in jazz studies.

It's very difficult to get into the pop world, and a certain element of luck is involved. Before you approach record companies, you need to gain as much experience as possible of playing or singing to audiences in clubs, colleges and dance halls, etc, and to find a manager to run your business affairs. But you could keep your group as a part-time venture, playing for local dances, etc, and combine that with a totally different daytime job. That's the way many bands and groups operate.

If your musical interests lie elsewhere than strictly classical or strictly pop, and you think you are suited to life in the Armed Forces, you could train as a **musician** with one of the regimental bands of the three armed services. You can join as a **junior bandsman** with a minimum of grade 5 standard as a normal entry requirement, or as an adult, provided you can demonstrate proficiency on your particular instrument. The Royal Air Force Music Services require grade 8 as a minimum standard entry. (See the B section of your careers library for fuller details of entry requirements, or contact the Forces' recruiting offices.)

Composing

There are very few people in the UK who make a living from composing. Most composers supplement their income by taking other work, such as teaching or music copying. Income from performance of works is very low, and royalties from records do not bring in much income either. Only about 90 living British 'classical' composers are listed in current record catalogues. Writing music for films, radio and TV is well paid, but getting established is not easy and luck is important, as well as talent. Most universities have facilities for postgraduate work in composition. Composition can be taken as a principal study, at either undergraduate or postgraduate level, at the music colleges: check prospectuses of individual colleges.

Conducting

Conducting is another extremely competitive area. College or university is essential, and an intending conductor should take every opportunity which occurs to conduct student orchestras, choirs, operatic societies, etc. He or she should apply for the various competitions for young conductors – details are published in *Music Journal*. A few orchestras offer trainee conductorships with the chance to understudy. Enquiries should be directed to all the orchestras, and to ballet and opera companies. There are a number of summer schools and short courses, and some postgraduate courses.

Teaching

The educational world offers more opportunities for musicians than any other occupational field. Musicians work in primary, middle, secondary and special schools; in colleges of music, colleges of further and higher education and universities; in music centres; and as private music teachers. Teachers of musical instruments can be appointed as **peripatetic** staff, visiting pupils in several schools. Anybody can set up as a **private music teacher**, but the most reputable have very good qualifications and are listed in the Incorporated Society of Musicians' Register of Professional Private Music Teachers. Successful **private teachers** can earn a comfortable living, but many find that much of their work is done at weekends and in the evenings, i.e. outside normal school and working hours. **Class teachers** in schools must be trained and qualified to teach. For graduates, this means taking a postgraduate certificate in education (PGCE) course, lasting one year, in order to obtain Qualified Teacher Status.

Broadcasting and TV

Music producers must have good qualifications, experience of organising and promoting music, and a very good knowledge of the musical repertoire. Most vacancies go to applicants already in broadcasting, or with experience in other aspects of the music business. **Sound balance** and **tape editing** are jobs sometimes open to new applicants. The bulk of jobs are with the BBC; there are limited opportunities with independent TV and radio.

Music journalism

There are very few openings for **music journalists** and **critics**. Contributors of articles and reviews on music to national newspapers tend to be musicologists, professional musicians, teachers, academics, and others with a name in the world of music. Their writing is in a freelance capacity. At a local level, covering concerts and other musical events would normally be only a small part of a reporter's job. There is also the specialist pop/rock press, where knowledge of the music as well as journalistic skills are most important.

Music libraries

Large orchestras, opera companies, schools of music and publishers have specialised music libraries. Many public libraries have specialist, qualified **librarians** to take charge of their collections of scores, records and musical literature. Academic libraries – in colleges and universities – offer opportunities too. The largest music library is in the BBC, where some 25 staff are employed (all qualified in music, though not necessarily in librarianship). Requirements vary – some employers, notably public libraries, will insist on librarianship qualifications, while others will be more interested in your knowledge of music. Music graduates can take a postgraduate qualification in librarianship (although grants for such a course are limited). Alternatively, you can take a first degree in librarianship.

Music publishing

This is a very specialised area, with a few opportunities for graduates. Most graduates currently working for music publishers are employed as editorial assistants, copyists and secretaries. **Editorial assistants** are generally concerned with the liaison between composer and printer, so that the scores are proofread, and brought into line with printing or copying practice. The **copyist** may not only correct composers' errors, but also do some arranging. Graduates may also work on a freelance basis, editing works for publication, proofreading and translating.

Retail

Musical knowledge can be very useful if you are selling things like pianos, guitars, classical or pop CDs, sheet music and scores. As for any shop work, you need to be good at dealing with people, especially with fussy and awkward customers: see *Selling, Retail & Distribution* in the *Just the Job!* series.

Music therapy

There are one-year postgraduate courses in music therapy, which is concerned with the treatment, education, rehabilitation and training, through music, of adults and children with physical, mental or emotional difficulties. Posts are available with local education authorities, social services departments and hospitals. (See later section on creative therapies for further details.)

Recording companies

There are very limited openings for music graduates in recording companies. Personal contacts, performance and musical activities are more important than paper qualifications. Graduates may find outlets for musical knowledge in manufacturing companies' production, promotion and distribution departments and as sales representatives.

COURSES AND COLLEGES

Music courses can be divided into graduate level courses, and those leading to licentiate or associate qualifications. Most graduate courses lead to either a degree (BMus) or a degree-equivalent graduate diploma. Graduate courses require a minimum of two A levels and five GCSEs at grade C. In addition, a high standard of musical ability is necessary; usually grade 8 on the main instrument and grade 5 or 6 on a second instrument. Non-graduate courses require a similar level of musical ability, but lower academic qualifications (five GCSEs at grade C – sometimes less for talented students).

Universities and colleges of higher education offer degree courses of two sorts: academic degrees and Bachelor of Education degrees for trainee teachers. BA or BMus degrees are academic degrees in which music history, methods of composition, musicology and such subjects are studied. Performance and composition may form part of some degrees. You should look at the CRAC *Degree Course Guide: Music* for further details. Trinity College of Music offers a BMus performance degree, which is a four-year, full-time integrated performance course, replacing the graduate level award.

Universities usually require three A levels, including music, for entry, while two may be acceptable for other institutions. There are a number of courses in other kinds of music than classical.

The ECCTIS computer database and *University and College Entrance Guide* are a good starting point to find the full range of courses.

It may be that, in certain universities, music students are expected to learn from an instrumental specialist designated by the university, rather than allowing the student to choose the tutor they have been learning with. Check with the universities if this concerns you.

BEd courses are intended for those who wish to teach music in schools, although a BA or BMus with a further year's postgraduate certificate in education would also be acceptable. Minimum entry requirements are two A levels plus five GCSEs at grade C (including mathematics and English). One of the A levels should normally be music.

Awards for advanced courses in music

Students on degrees or HNDs are normally eligible for mandatory awards. Lower-level courses at schools and colleges of music only rate discretionary awards. Discretionary awards for music courses are normally for three years only, though fourth-year awards are sometimes made to keyboard and string players, and singers at music colleges. Graduates usually find it difficult to get an award for further instrumental or vocal studies at music college.

DANCE & DANCE TEACHING

> For those with a love of, and a special aptitude for, dance there are two main career prospects – performing and teaching. There are several options for performers, but, for all of them, you need to be very talented. To teach dance, you need a degree or a professional qualification.

Performance

Like all the performing arts, dancing is an overcrowded profession. Dancers have an additional problem not shared by actors or musicians: even if they are successful, their career is short. In any type of dance, few dancers go on beyond the age of 35. Many don't even work to that age, if a serious or recurring injury forces them to stop. They have to be fit, well-trained and look right: there are limited opportunities for a six-foot ballerina or a five-foot premier male dancer! Modern dance has less rigid requirements concerning height, but physical attractiveness and physique can, nevertheless, play an important role.

For a performance career, training is provided by the independent dance schools. A list of accredited courses can be obtained from the Council for Dance Education and Training (see Further Information section). Competition for places is fierce, and grants are very difficult to obtain.

Classical ballet

Ballet dancers start very young. Unless you have already begun serious training by the age of sixteen, you are unlikely to succeed.

Full-time vocational courses (2–3 years) usually start at 16, after which a student would audition for ballet companies. The Royal Ballet School has a particular function in providing dancers for the Royal Ballet companies. Other schools, including the Central School of Ballet, offer training for wider careers opportunities. A very few dancers move on to **choreography**.

Contemporary and theatre dance
This includes all sorts of stagework, from experimental modern dance to musicals and the chorus line in pantomime, working in clubs, on cruise ships and in pop videos. Television offers a limited range of work for experienced dancers who have generally had an apprenticeship in stagework. Training is important, but does not require such an early start as with ballet. You can even start in your early twenties, especially if you are male. Contemporary and theatre dancers have often had ballet training at some stage.

Students of established dance schools are the ones most likely to find work. Dancers, like actors, must have an Equity card to work in mainstream professional theatre, film and television. Equity is the performers' union and controls entry to these areas of work. Trained dancers may find it easier to get work than actors.

Ballroom dancing
The way into ballroom dancing as a professional is via amateur competitions. A few dancers can make a professional career, but usually only for a limited period. Teaching is the main source of work. Other areas of employment within the field of ballroom dancing include organising competitions and providing various support services, usually on a part-time basis.

Community dance
The work involves developing dance within a particular geographical area through teaching or creating dance, or organising

others to do so. A full-time dance training or recognised dance teaching qualification is generally required. A full-time community dance course is offered at the Laban Centre, London: further information can be obtained from the Community Dance and Mime Foundation (see Further Information section).

Teaching dance

A range of opportunities exists, both as a private teacher and in independent and state schools. Dance teachers work with people of all ages and both sexes – from three-year-olds who are learning ballet, tap, etc, up to adults wishing to learn ballroom dancing, modern dance, or dance as a means of exercise. All teachers of dance should be good communicators and enjoy teaching, if they are to be successful. Teaching is not just a second best for those who fail to make the grade as performers.

For private teaching, a high standard of personal performance and good appropriate qualifications, such as teacher training at a vocational school or professional qualifications from one of the teaching societies, are necessary, combined with a good business sense and capital if you want to run your own school.

For teaching in state schools, a full teacher training is necessary, with the emphasis not so much on performing, as on dance as education and movement studies. To start training, you must normally have two A levels/Advanced GNVQ, plus supporting GCSEs at grade C, including English and maths.

DANCE COURSES IN FURTHER AND HIGHER EDUCATION

Some colleges of higher education offer degrees in human movement or performing arts, and some universities – such as the universities of Middlesex, Brighton, Birmingham, Leicester, Liverpool John Moores and Surrey – offer degrees in dance. Dance degree courses are also offered at Bretton Hall College and Roehampton Institute. As well as practical dance, these courses have an academic content, including such things as the physiology of movement and sociology of dance. In the main, these are not intended as courses for professional performers, but rather as general education or for intending teachers. Course information can be found in *University and College Entrance* and the *Compendium of Higher Education*, which should be in school and college careers libraries, careers service and public libraries. Many colleges offer BTEC Higher National Diplomas in performing arts, which include dance.

Degrees in dance, as well as three-year vocational training courses, are also offered at London Contemporary Dance School, the College of the Royal Academy of Dancing, London College of Dance, and the Laban Centre. These courses are much more practically based, and many graduates would go on to careers as performers and dance teachers.

Other opportunities with dance

Choreography – involves creating new dances. It can be studied as an option on many vocational training courses. Consult the prospectuses of the various institutes for further information.

Notation – the recording of dance movements, using symbols to represent the detailed position of the body at any one moment. It is used mostly for recording and rehearsal purposes. There are two main systems – Benesh Movement Notation and Labanotation.

Dance therapy – the use of movement and dance as a medium through which people with physical, mental and emotional difficulties can express themselves and develop (see later section on creative therapies).

DRAMA & ACTING

Careers in drama and acting are competitive, demanding and often insecure, but many people think of an acting career as something challenging and rewarding which they would love to do. Very few people become famous – but stardom is not everyone's goal. Training at drama college usually requires A levels, or their equivalent, or a degree.

Professional acting

Actors must be dedicated and they need plenty of stamina. Acting is a particularly disciplined business. As well as memorising lines and movements, actors may have to change their accent, posture and appearance. Come what may, the actors must be ready when the curtain goes up, and rehearsals must never be missed unless you are at death's door! The unreliable actor or actress is the one who doesn't get the job. A high degree of responsibility towards fellow performers and to the production is always essential.

Most actors will experience long periods of unemployment, long and unsocial hours, and poor levels of pay. All actors need to be prepared to face lots of rejections in their career.

GETTING STARTED

To act in theatre and television it is advisable to belong to Equity, the actor's union. Most employers have casting agreements with Equity. This means that they will engage only those performers who have previous professional experience, and who are usually members of the union, or an agreed quota of new-comers. This doesn't make work easy to get, but it does ensure that certain minimum standards of pay and conditions can be maintained and that a minimum standard of ability can be demanded.

If you want to act in films, television, radio, repertory theatre or in London's West End, the easiest way to get started is by the drama school route. Taking a course accredited by the National Council for Drama Training (see Further Information section) at a drama school means that you are registered with Equity and get a provisional Equity card which lasts for two years. Students from unaccredited courses, and those without training, may find it much more difficult to break in. Other ways include becoming a chorus singer or a dancer, or getting into one of the small alternative fringe and children's theatre companies. However, working for a non-Equity company leaves you without protection and open to exploitation.

Opportunities

- **Television** offers opportunities for leading and supporting roles, walk-on and 'extra' parts, stunt work and commercials.
- **Regional** repertory theatres, small-scale touring companies and theatre-in-education companies provide another source of employment. This area of work makes large demands in terms of performance skills and dedication. Some companies offer fairly secure long-term contracts; others have insecure profit-sharing (or loss-sharing!) arrangements.
- **Theatres** in major cities, including London's West End, may depend mainly on public or private subsidy. Economic pressures have affected the cast sizes and therefore job opportunities. Many young actors still start out in repertory companies which offer short seasons of farces, thrillers, contemporary plays and classics.

- **Films** offer limited opportunities. The UK film industry has been through several lean years, but there are signs of an upward trend in the British movie business.
- **Radio** drama still offers a lot of openings, at both national and regional level.
- Miscellaneous work includes dubbing, voice-overs and industrial training videos.

Other careers using drama

Drama is generally regarded as one of the performing arts, but there are many other opportunities besides performance in the theatre. These include production, stage management, administration, theatre-in-education, lighting, wardrobe, etc.

Drama teachers can work in both state-maintained and independent schools where drama is part of the curriculum. Many teachers of drama also offer another teaching subject, often English. There are opportunities in colleges of further education, universities and other higher education institutions, specialist drama schools, theatre groups, youth theatre workshops and arts centres.

There is also the use of drama as therapy. **Dramatherapists** use dramatic techniques to help patients with mental and physical handicaps and illnesses. Through drama, patients can express aspects of their problems which they are unable to do in their day-to-day lives. Drama therapy is only a small profession and therapists may be employed on a part-time basis, having to work in several different places to get a full workload. (See later section on creative therapies.)

EDUCATION AND TRAINING

There are two main routes for drama training – attending a drama school or following a degree course at a college or university. Most courses are broad and include voice, mime and

television technique. Entry requirements usually include A levels or a BTEC National in performing arts. There are specialised courses in directing and stage management.

BTEC National Diplomas in Performing Arts

Courses are now offered by many further education colleges. These are two-year courses, equivalent in standard to A levels, and normally requiring four GCSEs at grade C for entry. They are vocationally and practically based.

Drama schools

There are only a few drama schools in Britain and competition for places is intense. Normal entry varies between 17 and 25 years old. Exact requirements vary, but a good general education would be required, with many students having two A levels or a BTEC National in performing arts. Selection depends on an entrance audition. The more experience you have before going to drama school, the better will be your chance of getting a place. Courses usually last between two and three years.

Degrees

Students who wish to take a degree (including drama/theatre studies, diploma in dramatic art, or a recognised course for teachers) must have the appropriate entry qualifications. These are normally five GCSEs at grade C, with two subjects at A level – other equivalents are often acceptable. To train as a teacher in state schools, you must also have GCSE at grade C in mathematics and English. Competition for places on degree courses that include drama is very high.

Graduates of drama courses may need further training in a drama school before they can expect to start work.

There are a few postgraduate courses in, for instance, writing plays, production, design and criticism. Two or three drama schools offer courses for the teaching of drama, in conjunction with colleges of higher education.

Grants

Although there are drama schools that are recognised by the Department for Education and Employment, there are not necessarily grants available for these courses. Potential applicants are advised to check with their own local authority and the individual drama school. There are now some degree-level courses at drama schools which attract mandatory grants, as do teacher training courses. However, for non-degree courses, it is now almost impossible to get a discretionary award from your local authority, and the majority of students have to pay their way through training. If you are trying to be assessed for an award to study drama, remember that you can only apply to attend a recognised drama school, and that an interview with your local authority may be necessary to convince them that you are suitable.

Adults: note that maturity and previous experience may mean that stated entry requirements can be relaxed.

CIRCUS & STUNT WORK

W orking in a circus is more than just a job: it is a way of life and involves joining a very close-knit community. Most circuses tour in the UK or sometimes abroad, so performers and support staff are always on the move.

Circus and stunt performers need to keep fit and healthy. Much time is spent training and practising. An injury, poor health or just getting older may end a career and alternative employment will need to be sought.

Working in circuses

One of the fascinating things about traditional circuses is that many of the performers have been born into the business. They have been jugglers since childhood, have walked on slack-wires almost since they could stand, and have been taught their skills by family members. As a result, outsiders find it difficult to break in to this tight-knit community, even if they have the skills and talent. They may find it easier to obtain employment on the variety stage.

Unlike the traditional tented circus, there is now a New Circus movement which uses traditional jugglers, acrobats and tightrope walkers, but no animals. New Circus is more related to performing arts than traditional circus; performances may take place in arts centres, pubs, clubs and in the street. A one-year foundation course in New Circus skills is available at

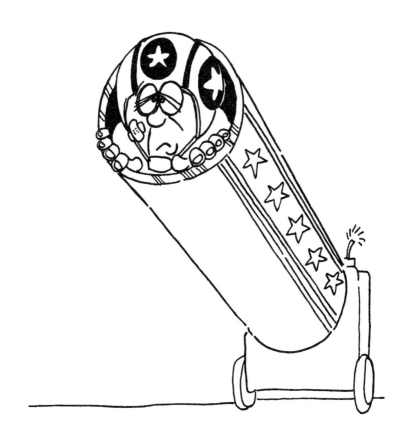

'Circomedia' in Bristol − *'the academy of circus arts and physical theatre'* − as well as shorter courses and one-day workshops.

A circus also needs a **manager** with one/two **assistant managers**, a **publicity and advertising assistant** and **box office staff**. These jobs involve various tasks − planning circus venues, ordering fodder for the animals, making up pay packets, buying food and other supplies, obtaining permission to display posters on hoardings, arranging for the printing of programmes and selling tickets. Other jobs involve showing the public to their seats, and selling ices and programmes. The smooth running of the performance relies on the **ring crew**, who set up the props and equipment, erect the cages for animal acts and dismantle them later. There is also a team of **electricians** and several **spotlight operators**.

GETTING STARTED

Travelling circuses sometimes find it difficult to recruit and keep skilled technical staff because most people prefer to work in a settled spot rather than to move continually. This means there are sometimes vacancies for mechanics, lighting technicians and electricians and, occasionally, even opportunities for training. On the musical side, there may be the occasional openings for proficient instrumentalists. If all else fails, and you are still determined to get into the circus, you might find a job as a **driver** or **tent mover**. This is hard, heavy work.

Instrumentalists and performers are not normally engaged locally. Acts are booked through a London agent who is in touch with performers all over the world. Other jobs can be found by approaching individual circuses.

Stunt work

There are only about 150 stunt performers in Britain – are you interested in joining them? You have to be both performer and technician, with a range of skills which include driving, parachuting, riding, gymnastics, martial arts and diving. Since stunt performers not only do stunts, but set them up and check the equipment to be used, they need to have a good technical understanding of what is going on. To do this work, you have to be very fit and active, with fast reactions. Remember that it is a short working life. When you feel yourself slowing down, you have to look around for something else, such as stunt arranging and coordination.

There is an Equity stunt register which film and television producers use. Applicants who want to get on to the register must be members of Equity, between 18 and 30, with recent qualifications in a range of skills. For information on specific qualifications and requirements write to Equity (see Further Information section). Be wary of employers looking for non-register performers. They are looking for daredevil types and this is where accidents can happen. However, even if you are on the register, don't expect insurance companies to welcome you with open arms!

GETTING STARTED

There is absolutely no formal way of getting into this type of work. Get as wide a range of skills as you can and perhaps try getting a job as an assistant with a stunt firm. You may find some addresses in *Contacts*, published by Spotlight.

TEACHING ENGLISH & DRAMA

There are jobs for teachers of English in all secondary schools and colleges, and many institutions also employ drama teachers. Some schools regard drama as a branch of English and prefer their staff to get involved in both areas. English is always one of the largest departments, as it is a core subject within the National Curriculum, whilst drama is much smaller. New entrants to teaching are virtually all graduates.

Primary schools

Although primary schools don't have jobs for people who *just* teach English or drama, there are plenty of opportunities to work with children on language and communication skills. In primary schools, *every* teacher is an English teacher, and drama is an important way of helping children to learn and develop. Some specialisation is possible: you may see jobs advertised for teachers wanting to take special responsibility for 'language' in primary and middle schools. This means being the school's 'expert' on that area of work, a resource upon which the other members of staff can draw, and you might be paid at a higher point on the salary scale. To be selected for that sort of post, you would need to be an experienced teacher and to have attended various in-service training courses, for example on techniques of teaching reading.

Secondary schools

In secondary schools, teaching English and/or drama can cover a very wide range of activities. One lesson might be with a group of thirty eleven-year-olds, talking about writing stories; the next period, you might have a much smaller class doing A level English literature, or theatre studies. Then there is all the GCSE teaching for Years 10 and 11 – and 'retake' classes in the sixth form for people who are anxious to improve their GCSE grade. Some pupils will love your subject; some will hate it. But, whatever their feelings, it's the teacher's job to try to get the best from all pupils.

English is a very lively subject area. Although grammar and literature are still important components of English coursework, they are not the only topics! Because the subject concerns communication, English teachers can find themselves involved in all sorts of activities which you might not connect with English. For instance, English departments often help with work experience projects for older pupils – teaching pupils to write suitable letters to employers; developing their oral skills through discussion of their work experience; writing logbooks, diaries, summaries and so on. These days, a lot of use is made of information technology, too.

Drama plays an important role in helping pupils to develop self-confidence and imagination. It is not all that widely available as an examination subject in schools, and so there is less requirement for drama teachers than for many other subject areas. However, it's often a very popular subject and at sixth form level there seems to be a growing interest in A level courses such as theatre studies.

Colleges

In colleges of further education, the work of the teacher or lecturer is mainly directed towards preparing students for exams –

again, GCSE and A levels, and also subjects like English for business.

At more advanced levels, there are opportunities for teaching in universities and colleges of higher education. These are posts for academics who pursue their own research, as well as teaching students on degree and postgraduate courses.

GETTING STARTED IN TEACHING

Teaching is now, for new entrants, generally an all-graduate profession, so you must have a degree, and there are two main routes.

- The Bachelor of Education (BEd), gained through a three-year or four-year honours degree course. This is the more popular entry route for primary teachers.
- Most secondary teachers take a first degree in the subject they wish to teach, followed by a postgraduate certificate in education (PGCE). The first degree must be appropriate to the curricular work in schools and colleges.

To be accepted on a degree course, school/college-leavers usually require:

- a minimum of two A levels (or the equivalent);
- supporting GCSEs, which must include English and maths at grades A–C;
- for students born on or after 1 September 1979, a GCSE in a science subject (grade A–C) is required for entry to primary teacher training from September 1998.

Adults with few or no qualifications wanting to train for teaching could follow an Access course. These courses are offered at many further education colleges and are designed as an alternative to GCSEs and A levels for entry to degree and other HE courses (minimum age for entry varies between 21 and 24 years). Admissions tutors may look for school subject relevance in A levels or in the Access course content.

Note: All applicants to teacher training are expected to have GCSE grade C or above in both English and mathematics (or equivalent). Some colleges will allow applicants over 25 to take an entrance test if they have had no opportunity to gain such exam passes.

In the area of drama, besides the above routes, there are various courses at specialist drama colleges; but you would still need to take a teacher training course if you wanted to teach in a state school.

Mature entrants to teaching can enter by different routes, such as the shortened two-year BEd course, or through the licensed teacher scheme.

just
THE
JOB

BACKSTAGE THEATRE WORK

There are many jobs 'behind the scenes' in a theatre, all essential to the success of a production. These include costume, make-up, lighting and music, theatre design, as well as stage management and production. Some jobs require theatre experience as well as academic and professional qualifications; all the areas of work require a lot of stamina and determination!

Although directors and designers earn good salaries when they are working, most technical jobs in the theatre are not particularly well paid. The majority of technicians rely on the large amounts of essential overtime to boost their earnings. Working hours are long and involve much evening and some night work. You will find below a short description of the jobs and some information on training, but further research on your part will be necessary to gather more detailed information. Any experience you can gain in amateur theatre productions is always useful.

NVQs in Stagecraft
These qualifications are now available for people already working or training backstage in the theatre or in performing arts. They cover lighting, flying (controlling scenery and equipment from the space above the stage), costumes and scenery at NVQ levels 1 or 2, and are assessed at a few selected centres.

Director
The director puts the whole show together, combining and

controlling the work of actors, writers, musicians, singers, dancers and backstage workers. The job requires creativity and organising ability. Training opportunities with theatre companies are very limited and most young directors are graduates, often of drama or performing arts courses which may include directing, although not necessarily. The Rose Bruford College offers a three-year BA(Hons) degree course in directing, for which you should receive a mandatory grant. The Arts Council funds eight traineeships per year for those with some experience in theatre directing, including two places specifically for black or Asian directors.

Producer

The producer raises the money for the show, and generally ensures that it actually happens. In the commercial theatre, the producer usually starts with finding the backers for a production, followed by arranging hire of a theatre, suitable performers and a director. There is no formal training but a background in arts administration could be useful.

Stage manager

The stage manager coordinates the work of the whole backstage team, keeping rehearsals and performances running smoothly. Because of the large team, the theatre has to be a highly disciplined place and the stage manager is the person in charge. A good stage manager is always in demand and will not often be out of work. Stage management or technical theatre courses at various levels are available at a number of drama colleges and some institutions of further and higher education.

Production manager

The production manager assists the director and producer with general backstage administration, and represents the communication link between the actors and technicians and the company management. Production managers usually have a stage management background.

Assistant stage manager

The assistant stage manager helps with jobs like getting props, playing-in taped sound effects, prompting, making tea and 10,000 other useful little tasks. ASMs would usually have done either stage management or acting training.

Stagehand

The stagehand moves all the items on the stage which are not properties (props) or electrics. Furniture and chunks of scenery are their responsibility, but *not* anything the actors carry – fans, teacups, revolvers and so forth. A theatre will have a small group of resident stagehands and will take on extra staff when needed, and this is an area of work where it is possible to get a foot in the door.

Dresser

The dresser looks after wigs and costumes, helps actors dress for the performance and generally assists them. A dresser could combine this job with being a **wardrobe assistant**. Dressers are not necessarily trained, but see **wardrobe master/ mistress**, below.

Properties

The properties manager makes sure that all the 'props' are there for the performance and put back at the end of the show. During rehearsals, all the necessary items are bought, borrowed or made and, during the run, are repaired or replaced as necessary. There are courses in property-making at various drama and further education colleges up to degree level.

Costume designer

The costume designer designs and superintends the costumes for

AND THIS IS YOUR MAGIC CARPET

the production. He/she decides whether costumes should be newly made, hired or modified from stock. The job does not usually include the practical work of sewing, but it is concerned with producing the working sketches and drawings for the wardrobe department. A designer needs to be able to research costumes of different times and places. A course in fashion design would provide a useful background. Alternatively, there are specialist courses in costume design and theatre wardrobe.

Wardrobe master/mistress

This involves making, altering and maintaining the costumes. In a rep theatre, the job also involves looking after the costume store, which can be quite large. The work can be very pressured, with deadlines which must be met. Practical skills are very important, particularly the ability to translate drawings into a finished product. A good knowledge of materials is required. There are full-time BTEC HND and degree courses, BTEC National and college diploma courses at many theatre schools.

Wardrobe assistant

Wardrobe assistants help with the routine sewing, ironing and cleaning of costumes. A wardrobe assistant must have good practical skills and be quick and flexible.

Make-up

In theatre, actors generally do their own make-up, so opportunities for make-up assistants may be few and far between. However, make-up artists, working in the theatre in another capacity, may be called upon for advice. There are more opportunities in television and film. Several FE colleges offer diploma courses in theatrical make-up, or it may be included as an option in more general beauty and make-up courses.

Set designer

The set is designed and plans are produced, with working drawings and models from which it will be made. Some set designers might also design the costumes, to achieve an integrated effect. There are theatre design courses at degree and BTEC Higher National Diploma level. See *Art & Design* in the *Just the Job!* series for details.

Carpenter

The carpenter works in a workshop and on stage, making new sets and modifying and repairing old ones. Practical ability, with a strong interest in the theatre, is essential. It is not always necessary to be a skilled joiner or qualified carpenter. There is a full-time diploma course at RADA.

Scene painter

Scene painters work with the set designer and the carpenter producing the set. Scene painting is a rather specialised job, a craft rather than a creative process. RADA offers a diploma course.

Electrician

The electrician is responsible for all the electrical systems in the theatre, for lighting and power for technical equipment. It is sometimes possible to start as a trainee in a theatre, although an ordinary electrical installation training would be satisfactory. RADA offers a full-time course.

Lighting designer and technician

All the stage lighting requirements need designers and technicians. Starting as an electrician, technical knowledge is mainly acquired through experience. Advancements in electronics have greatly improved control systems. The **lighting technician** sits at the lighting console during the performance, taking cues from the stage manager. In larger theatres, the overall effect of the lighting will be organised by a **lighting designer**. A lighting designer would have worked his or her way up from lighting technician. It is a practical job where creative flair is needed as well as technical knowledge and qualifications.

Musical director and arranger

The musical director composes or arranges the music for a performance and teaches actors and singers (both soloists and choruses) their music. He or she may hire instrumentalists for an orchestra (although this job is done by an orchestra manager in professional and semi-professional companies) and, most importantly, conducts singers and musicians during the performance. This job demands a very experienced and competent musician. The majority of musical directors have had some years of training at music college, or have a pop or light music background.

Répétiteur/rehearsal pianist

This involves helping the singers to learn their music (by repetition) and playing for rehearsals. Similarly a ballet company will have a rehearsal pianist who plays for the dancers' class work and for rehearsals.

Choreographer

The choreographer arranges and composes in dance movements and steps. It's a creative job, usually done by someone who has been a dancer and has moved into choreography (see section on dance).

THEATRE ADMINISTRATOR

Theatre administration covers all the work and responsibilities which must be undertaken to ensure that everything is as it should be when the curtain goes up on a performance. The individuals involved in this work are the theatre manager, box office manager, publicity manager and marketing officer, and company manager. In small companies, it is possible to work your way up, but most theatre administrators have a degree or the equivalent.

Theatre administrators work in small teams planning the overall financial running of a theatre, trying to ensure that it is making a profit and not a loss. Decisions must be made about the overall policy of the theatre. What plays are to be performed? Is the programme well-balanced, and does it avoid offering either all farces and thrillers, or all experimental drama? Financial decisions must be made about such things as casting and production costs.

Besides these matters, there are also the day-to-day jobs of running the theatre. Tickets must be sold – and each seat only once! The show must be advertised, otherwise no seat would ever be sold. The theatre must be cleaned, the bar stocked and staffed, electricity bills have to be paid, and after the show someone must turn off the lights and check security.

In the United Kingdom there are four different sorts of theatres and theatrical companies:

The subsidised theatre

This includes the large national companies – the Royal Shakespeare, the National Theatre, English National Opera and so on – as well as the many local repertory theatres. These are companies partly financed by grants, but still dependent, of course, on filling seats. They run a more or less continuous programme and have permanent staff. A company like the National Theatre, with its three theatres, hundreds of staff and millions of pounds subsidy, needs a large administrative staff, including production managers, publicity and marketing staff, front-of-house managers and many others, each with a specialised function. A modest repertory company might have only two or three full-time administrative staff, each having to turn their hand to a range of jobs.

Theatres in arts complexes and centres

These are really part of the subsidised theatre. Depending on the size of an arts centre, an administrator might have overall responsibility for a centre, or responsibility for the theatre section alone. The range of duties could be much the same as in a repertory theatre company or possibly rather wider.

Touring companies

There is a mixture of companies involved in touring, putting on anything from large-scale orchestral works, operas, musicals and plays, to one-person shows. Some tour companies are run on a purely commercial basis, while others are subsidised. Company managers have to arrange venues, negotiate fees, arrange transport and accommodation, pay bills and generally ensure that all aspects run smoothly.

Commercial theatres

These are private theatres owned by individuals, companies and trusts, relying entirely on box office receipts to make ends meet. Owners earn money by letting their theatre to production companies who select the play and the players and take the financial risk of failure.

In the commercial theatre there are two areas of management. It is possible to work for a theatre-owning company engaging performers (as individuals or companies), maintaining the theatre and running the front-of-house services (box office and catering). Alternatively, administrators can work as **company managers**, involved in raising finance for a company, negotiating performing rights, dealing with performers' contracts, hiring a stage crew and managing publicity.

GETTING STARTED

Theatre administration is a small profession, in which people start their career in many different ways. The most conventional route nowadays is by taking a degree (not necessarily in drama) and getting involved with organising student theatre, then following this with postgraduate training in arts administration; although there are HNDs and a few degrees in arts administration/management. Other routes might be via business studies or accounting courses and work on the finance side of theatre administration. Consult higher education course handbooks, or the ECCTIS database in your local careers centre library. Some theatre administrators are actors who have moved into running a company.

An increasing number of further education colleges are now offering the two-year BTEC National Diploma in performing arts. Arts administration is one of the options on this course, for which four GCSEs at grade C, including English, are required.

LOOKING FOR JOBS

Jobs are advertised in *The Stage* and in the *Guardian* arts and media jobs section (the Saturday and Monday editions). Over a few weeks, the *Guardian* will give you a good idea of the sort of jobs which come up and the salaries which are being offered, particularly in the area of subsidised theatre. The annual entertainment directory *Contacts* gives addresses of most theatres and theatrical companies in Great Britain. It can be obtained from Spotlight Publishers.

ARTS ADMINISTRATOR

Arts administrators are practical people. They administer cultural activities such as theatre, music and the visual arts. They are good organisers and communicators. They manage people, programmes of future activities, buildings and finances, making sure that everything runs smoothly, whether they work in a multi-purpose leisure centre or a theatre. There are opportunities ranging from jobs requiring only a few GCSEs, to those requiring a degree or equivalent qualification.

There are jobs with:

- theatrical, opera and dance companies;
- orchestras and musical ensembles;
- theatres, concert halls, art galleries;
- local authority entertainments departments;
- arts centres;
- community theatre workshops;
- theatre-in-education companies.

What the work involves

Each job is different. You might work for an organisation which offers a touring performance programme, like many theatrical or dance companies, or for one which hires artists and puts on events. But, wherever you work, you are likely to get involved in things like:

- programme planning;

- publicity and promotional activities;
- liaison with printers and designers;
- financial management, staff salaries and perhaps fund-raising;
- booking performers and instrumentalists;
- organising the artists' contracts;
- tour and travel arrangements;
- accommodation and, perhaps, provision of meals and refreshments;
- building maintenance contracts and safety regulations;
- in some types of work, sitting on committees and going to meetings.

In a small organisation, one person could be responsible for all these jobs. In larger organisations, where more than one administrator is employed, there is greater specialisation of tasks.

What it takes

An arts administrator needs to be:

- highly literate and numerate;
- a good organiser, who is very efficient and calm in a crisis;
- tactful and sensitive;
- able to organise people who may resent being 'organised';
- good at working in a team;
- willing to work irregular and unsocial hours;
- adaptable and flexible.

Ben – arts centre administrator

' I've always been interested in the arts – everything from Shakespeare to Spike Lee. I don't know where I got it from. Both my parents are very down to earth, and they think the arts are a waste of time!

I enjoyed drama, music and art at school. Maybe if I'd really concentrated on one area, I might have been a performer or artist instead of an administrator. I'll never know! I did pretty well in my GCSEs, so I went on into the sixth form and took A levels. I thought of going to university to do a degree in art history, but eventually decided to do a more vocational course. I chose a Higher National Diploma in business studies, which included leisure amenities management.

I used to be involved in a local drama group, and during the college holidays I helped out at the theatre that we used. This was really useful experience. I worked in the box office and as an usher, and they even let me loose on designing a poster when they realised I was keen on art.

When I completed my course, the theatre offered me a clerical job which was mostly financial work. I took it, while I carried on looking for something better. I saw an ad for assistant manager of this centre. I took a lot of trouble over my application, because I knew competition would be tough. A good reference from the theatre helped a lot. I got the job and I love it. There's so much variety – marketing, booking performers, organising exhibitions, personnel and financial work. I even help behind the bar when we're busy. The only drawback is the evening and weekend work, but you get used to planning your life around that. The pay is probably less than for a manager in commerce or industry, but it's enough.

Naima, the manager, did a postgraduate qualification in arts administration. She's very encouraging and lets me take a lot of responsibility. Before long, I hope to be managing a theatre or arts centre myself. Who knows, one day I might be running the Barbican Centre or the Edinburgh Festival . . .

PAY

In the early stages of your career, you are likely to be very lowly paid, even if you are a graduate. There are two reasons for this. Many of the organisations employing arts administrators are themselves poor, perhaps dependent on fund-raising activities for their finance. The other reason is that this is a competitive area of work to get into, and there are many people keen to do the jobs which will give you a foothold into the arts administration world. If you become successful at arts administration, and get one of the top jobs – e.g. administrator of the Royal Opera House or the Barbican – then you will be very well paid. There are also a certain number of middle-range jobs, particularly in local authority arts administration.

PROSPECTS

For a good overview of the job possibilities, you should look at the *Guardian*'s 'Creative and Media' vacancies in Monday and Saturday editions. Other sources of job adverts include *The Stage* and regional daily papers. These will give you a picture of the types of jobs available, and what you would be expected to do.

Some typical job advertisements

Press and Marketing Officer: '*As a young people's theatre company, we are now embarking on the most exciting development in our history, following a National Lotteries Arts Award. In order to maximise our national profile, we now seek an experienced press officer to join our busy marketing department.*'

Administrator: '*Dance Agency in London. £14,349–£15,629 initially 2-year fixed term. Key areas of responsibility include administration of finance, personnel, company business, computer network, office organisation and support for the Director. A good aptitude for computers and a keenness to develop skills in this area, plus efficiency and thoroughness, are essential.*'

Press Officer: '*Dance Company. circa £18k. Britain's biggest and most exciting contemporary dance company seeks a press officer to join its highly motivated and successful marketing team. The press officer will be a key member of the team, closely involved in supporting sponsors and funders, and promoting the company's extensive education and outreach work. We seek a press officer who can maintain and develop our profile with the arts media, and broaden coverage to embrace lifestyle and general interest print and broadcast media.*'

Marketing Manager: '*One of Britain's leading touring theatre companies seeks a marketing manager to further develop the strategic marketing, promotion and corporate identity of the company. Previous arts marketing experience is essential. Salary: c £17,500.*'

Administrative Assistant – Dance Tours: '*An international sports and arts management organisation is offering an exciting opportunity for someone with a keen interest in, and knowledge of, classical and contemporary dance to work in a vital support role on promoting, planning and implementing international tours for our dance company clients. All applicants must speak good French and German and be highly organised under pressure. Enthusiasm for the subject matter must be further complemented by strong administrative skills, typing, computer literacy, numeracy. Candidates with experience of touring, planning and budgeting or arts administration preferred.*'

Assistant Administrator: '*sought by London children's theatre company. Salary £10,600. Apply in writing with CV.*' (No further details provided.)

EDUCATION AND TRAINING

There is no simple list of qualifications to acquire if you want to get into arts administration. Many people in this work are arts graduates who have degrees in subjects like art history, music, or drama, any of which would be suitable for this work, although degrees in other disciplines, such as finance or marketing, would be very acceptable. In fact, there is a range of higher education courses available, giving rise to an increase in job applicants with good qualifications including HNDs and post-graduate diplomas. However, there are people, especially in the community arts field, who have arrived at their jobs by other routes, and may have no educational qualifications at all.

Adults may find that experience in other areas of administration, public relations, etc, together with an active interest in the arts, may outweigh the advantages of formal educational qualifications.

For school-leavers and college-leavers, however, it would be highly desirable to offer at least A levels, an Advanced GNVQ or equivalent qualifications, to stand any chance of being considered for jobs, and serious thought should be given to taking a degree. This will train you in expressing yourself with clarity, and widen your horizons and knowledge. However, non-academic activities, such as organising functions and running societies, would give you experience and skills directly applicable to arts administration.

Secretarial and computer skills are very useful, and computer literacy is increasingly mentioned in job adverts.

It is very important to gain any practical experience you can of work with arts organisations – see if your local arts centre could do with voluntary help. If you are interested in this type of work, then it's likely that you already have local contacts in the arts, which you may be able to use.

Courses
The Arts Council publishes useful information on courses, and runs short courses at regional training centres.

There are full-time degree and BTEC HND courses in Arts Management. There are part-time diploma courses in Arts

Administration. There are other short and part-time courses, including the work-based assessment projects in Leisure and Amenity Management (arts administration option) run by the Institute of Leisure and Amenity Management.

At a lower level, GNVQ courses in Performing Arts are gradually being phased in. Other possibilities are the GNVQs in Leisure Studies, which cover business skills applied to various sectors of the leisure industry, including arts and entertainment, and cultural recreation. The Advanced GNVQ course can be a bridge to higher education for those who favour a vocational approach to the subject.

BETTING & GAMING

Whatever some people may think about the morality of betting and gaming, most of us enjoy a little flutter now and then. This may take the form of filling in a pools coupon each week, playing bingo, buying lottery tickets, placing an occasional each-way bet on a horse we like the name of, or regularly visiting race tracks and casinos. In all these industries, there are jobs for people with all levels of qualifications. The minimum age for working in betting shops and casinos is 18.

The gaming industry is strictly controlled, through inspectors, by the Gaming Board of Great Britain. Casino staff and bingo club managers must hold a Certificate of Consent from the Gaming Board, for which a clean record is essential. The Home Office is responsible for the betting side of the industry.

Betting

Betting (horse and greyhound races, etc) is carried out in betting shops and on the course/track through bookies and the Tote. Only about 10% of horse-race bets are actually placed on course.

There are three large employers, with between 800 and 2000 shops each and representatives who take on-course bets – Coral Racing, Ladbrokes, and William Hill. These take half the bets placed. The Horserace Totalisator Board (The Tote) has about 200 shops. The Tote is responsible to the Home Office and profits go back into racing through payments to the Horserace

Levy Board, racecourses and sponsorship. The Tote's permanent staff for on-course or track work number only about 70, the great majority of whom are part-time. Other bets are placed through small firms (often family businesses) who operate in shops and on course.

TRAINING SCHEMES

Bookmakers
Most large firms have training schemes for the people who work alongside and assist managers of bookmakers' shops, settling bets throughout the day. These assistant managers are usually called *settlers*. People in their early twenties with good GCSEs or equivalent in maths and English are preferred. You need to be good at arithmetic and you may be asked to take a test when you apply for a job. Training takes place both on-the-job and through short courses at the firm's training school. You can expect to become the manager of a betting shop within 6–18 months of commencing training.

Counter clerks and payout clerks
There are no specific entry requirements. Experience of shop work, especially as a cashier, could be useful.

On-course/track staff
These are usually recruited from experienced betting shop staff.

The Tote
There is limited recruitment of school-leavers, but they would consider young people over 18 with two GCSEs at grade C or equivalent for course or betting shop work.

Bingo clubs and centres
There are nearly 1000 licensed bingo clubs. Most **club managers** are fairly young. Young people under 18 can work in bingo clubs – as usherettes, etc, provided they do not take part

in the gaming. Large bingo clubs have trainee assistant manager schemes – the usual age is 20–21. Good GCSEs or equivalent are useful but not essential. You need to be confident and extrovert, and an entertainment background, or experience of contact with the public, is an advantage. Enthusiasm and commitment are important. There is a combination of on- and off-the-job training. Promotion is to deputy manager and then to manager. Successful trainees can expect to become managers in about three years.

Casinos

There are over 100 casinos in the country, employing about 4000 staff. Most of the money is taken in the larger London clubs.

A **croupier** runs each individual game, taking in the bets and paying out the winnings. Most croupiers are under 30: the minimum age for employment is 18. There is usually a shortage of croupiers because of high staff turnover. Several major casino operators have training schemes for croupiers/dealers. There are no specific entry requirements, but you should be good at arithmetic and have manual dexterity and be prepared to work night shifts. Appearance and personality are very important. A 'clean record' is essential. For experienced croupiers there are good opportunities to work abroad. The British Casino Association (see Further Information section) publishes lists of casino addresses.

Cruise ships often have a casino where croupiers are needed. Casino concessions are run by outside concerns, such as Southern Games and VIP International (see Further Information section).

Pools promoters

There are three firms in the pools business, with their offices mainly in the north. Vernons and Littlewoods are the biggest. School-leavers are accepted as pools clerks. A good general education is required, with a reasonable standard of arithmetic. Training is given on-the-job.

CREATIVE THERAPIES

> The creative therapies include opportunities for specialists in dance, drama, music and art. They work in a variety of settings such as hospitals, clinics, special schools and prisons, helping patients to express themselves and communicate.

Creative activities have a useful role as a form of therapy or treatment for people who have difficulty in expressing themselves, or who need a stimulus to help them take part in activities. Psychiatric patients, children with emotional difficulties or people with learning difficulties can sometimes only communicate freely through art, drama or music. Other patients, with medical problems, may benefit from the exercise of painting, playing a musical instrument, or taking part in drama, dance or other artistic expression.

Posts in the creative therapies are rather scarce and not highly paid, with part-time and sessional work being more usual than full-time posts. Many therapists carry out their work within an existing job, such as nursing, teaching, psychology or occupational therapy.

All creative therapy involves very demanding work, especially where psychiatric or emotionally disturbed patients are concerned. The therapist must develop a relationship with patients which will help them to express their feelings through the medium being used. The strength of feelings shown can make the therapist feel very involved with patients, making it difficult to leave the working day behind.

Because it requires great sensitivity and maturity, working in creative therapy is really a career for experienced adults, rather than for school- or college-leavers. Young people should start by getting training in the particular art form they want to use.

Adults: note that maturity and previous experience may mean that stated entry requirements can be relaxed.

Art therapy

Art therapists often work with emotionally disturbed or non-communicative patients, in child guidance clinics or psychiatric units. They try to develop a close relationship which will help patients express themselves and come to a better understanding of themselves. A patient's work can be kept as a record of development which can be referred to by the patient, therapist or other colleagues at any time.

Art therapists work in both private and local authority special schools, guidance and psychotherapy clinics, psychiatric hospitals, occupational therapy departments of hospitals, units for disturbed adolescents, prisons, etc.

TRAINING

Training is open to graduates in art or design or qualified professionals such as teachers or therapists who have artistic ability. Mature, flexible people are needed, with at least a year's experience of work in the health service, education or community. It is possible to study for a degree in art therapies rather than follow the postgraduate route, although places are very limited.

Music therapy

Music therapy mainly involves work with adults and children suffering from physical, mental or emotional difficulties, rather than physical illnesses, though there are some opportunities with elderly people, in hospices, and with prisoners. The therapist is likely to work not only with individuals but also with groups. Posts are available with education authorities, independent special schools, social services departments, prisons and hospitals. Therapists may be employed full-time, part-time, or on a sessional basis.

TRAINING

The first step is normally to gain qualifications in music (degree or diploma) and then take a music therapy course (details available from the British Society for Music Therapy). There may be openings for people with other professional qualifications, such as psychology, general or special needs teaching, etc, but you would still need a high level of musicianship (gained through spare-time activities, for instance). Note that if you want to work in local education authority schools as a music therapist, you will usually need to have a teaching qualification. There are postgraduate full-time music therapy courses in the UK.

Dance therapy

As with the other creative therapies, the work is mainly with adults and children with learning difficulties, psychiatrically ill patients and elderly people, either in the community or as part of a team in a hospital. Therapists also work in the community with other groups, such as youth clubs and schools.

The Association of Dance Therapists (International) has set up a range of training courses (mainly by distance learning, supported by optional practical workshops). Those who have studied with the Association so far include nurses, physiotherapists, occupational and recreational therapists, psychologists, dance teachers and dance students. Holders of the Association's Diploma can do supervised voluntary work in hospitals, if they are not in a job which enables them to get experience.

TRAINING

The Association of Dance Therapists (International) offers sessional work at beginners' level which can progress to the Basic Level Diploma. These studies are available for community as well as medical work, for students who want to add dance therapy to their existing skills. There are also follow-on studies for those working in the psychiatric sector, which can lead to the Intermediate Level Diploma. Because these courses are offered by a private organisation, and are on a part-time basis, you will not necessarily receive any financial help towards their costs. However, people already working for the NHS are likely to have their fees paid. The fees are, in any case, fairly modest.

There are some centres which offer postgraduate qualifications in dance and movement. There are also relevant full- and part-time courses in **eurythmy**, offered in association with the Rudolf Steiner Organisation – these entail a form of movement therapy based on Steinerian principles.

Dramatherapy

Dramatherapy is a technique usually used with groups rather than individuals. A dramatherapist might work with a group of disturbed adolescents, a group of prisoners or psychiatric patients, or with physically and mentally disabled people of all ages. Dramatherapy is also used with people who are not ill or seriously disturbed at all, but who want help in learning to express their emotions.

The aims of dramatherapy can be very wide-ranging. The therapist working with people with physical and/or mental disabilities might be trying to get them moving better, improving their balance and their speech, perhaps improving basic social and life skills. Role-play is often used to help patients express emotions such as anger and fear.

Rather than being a full-time profession, dramatherapy is often used by people already working in the health services (e.g. clinical psychologists, mental health nurses), education, psychotherapy or other counselling roles.

TRAINING

There are postgraduate training courses in dramatherapy. These courses are intended for people already using dramatherapy in their work, and they include theoretical and workshop study, as well as supervised work experience.

ASTROLOGY

A strologers believe that the positions and movements of the Sun and the planets in our solar system can be correlated to events on Earth, whether applied to the individual or to matters generally. In some societies, the astrologer plays an important role in business and industry as well as in personal matters. There are no specified entry qualifications for most astrology courses.

Increasingly, astrologers work in the counselling and psychotherapeutic fields, using the astrological model as a base of reference. Whether or not you think this model is reasonable, there are sufficient people who do to offer some opportunity of making a living out of this study.

Some astrologers offer a service to private clients through personal interviews or by post. Other opportunities may be available in journalism, teaching and lecturing.

Astrology may be an ancient art, but many astrologers now use computer software programs to help them in their calculations.

TRAINING

Astrology training is offered mainly through private organisations. Courses are offered by correspondence, workshops, seminars and summer schools. An example of one organisation is the Faculty of Astrological Studies, which offers correspondence courses, and face-to-face tuition in London, Glasgow and Bath.

There are no formal courses within the state sector of education, with the exception of evening classes offered by some local education authorities.

GRAPHOLOGY

Graphologists use handwriting analysis to draw conclusions about the personality of the writer. This sort of analysis is not just done for fun. Used in conjunction with other methods of assessment, it has many serious applications. There are no specific entry requirements to train in graphology.

Information derived from a graphological analysis can be used by firms in coming to a decision about appointing a new employee, to help someone who is trying to decide about their career, in personal counselling, and in a range of other situations.

Graphologists are usually self-employed and engaged as consultants when needed, and paid a fee for their work. They are more widely used in some other parts of the European Union than in Britain, particularly in employee recruitment. Closer European integration could mean that their use in this country will increase.

TRAINING

There are no known full-time courses for graphologists. There are, however, a number of part-time introductory courses offered through local adult education centres, and various other courses offered by the organisations listed at the end of this book, or by their individual members. The British Institute of Graphologists can provide information about tuition available, including correspondence courses, workshops and private tuition.

There are also many books published on graphology, and you might wish to study these to get an idea of whether it is a subject you wish to pursue more seriously.

The Tutorial Section of the International Graphology Association is an Accredited Correspondence College.

FOR FURTHER INFORMATION

Central Council of Physical Recreation – Francis House, Francis Street, London SW1P 1DE. Tel: 0171 828 3163.

Institute of Leisure and Amenity Management – ILAM House, Lower Basildon, Reading RG8 9NE. Tel: 01491 874222.

Institute of Sport and Recreation Management – Giffard House, 36–38 Sherrard Street, Melton Mowbray, Leicestershire LE13 1XJ. Tel: 01664 65531.

Keep Fit Association – Francis House, Francis Street, London SW1P 1DE. Tel: 0171 233 8898.

National Coaching Foundation – 114 Cardigan Road, Headingley, Leeds LS6 3BJ. Tel: 0113 2744 802.

Physical Education Association of the UK – Suite 5, 10 Churchill Square, Kingshill, West Malling, Kent ME19 4DU. Tel: 01732 875888. Publishes a booklet *A Career in Physical Education, Sport and Recreation.*

Sports Aid Foundation – 16 Upper Woburn Place, London WC1H 0QN. Tel: 0171 387 9380.

Sports Council Information Centre – 16 Upper Woburn Place, London WC1H 0QP. Tel: 0171 388 1277. Provides a careers information pack, which includes a courses guide and addresses of the sports' governing bodies.

Women's Sports Foundation – Wesley House, 4 Wild Court, London WC2B 4AU. Tel: 0171 831 7863.

Professional bodies associated with specific sports:
British Boxing Board of Control Ltd – Jack Petersen House, 52a Borough High Street, London SE1 1XW. Tel: 0171 403 5879.

British Canoe Union – Adbolton Lane, West Bridgford, Nottingham NG2 5AS. Tel: 0115 9821 100.

British Mountaineering Council – 177–179 Burton Road, West Didsbury, Manchester M20 2BB. Tel: 0161 445 4747.

British Sub-Aqua Club – Telford's Quay, Ellesmere Port, South Wirral, Cheshire L65 4FY. Tel: 0151 357 1951.

The Cricket Council – Lord's Cricket Ground, London NW8 8QN.

English Ski Council – Area Library Building, Queensway Mall, The Cornbow, Halesowen, West Midlands B63 4AJ. Tel: 0121 501 2314.

Footballers' Further Education and Vocational Training Society Ltd – 2 Oxford Court, Bishopsgate, Off Lower Mosley Road, Manchester M2 3WQ. Tel: 0161 236 0637.

Lawn Tennis Association – Queen's Club, West Kensington, London W14 9EG. Tel: 0171 381 7017.

National Association for Outdoor Education – 12 St. Andrew's Churchyard, Penrith, Cumbria CA11 7YE. Tel: 01768 65113.

National Cycling Centre – Manchester Velodrome, 1 Stuart Street, Manchester M11 4DQ. Tel: 0161 223 2244.

Outward Bound Trust – PO Box 1219, Windsor, Berks SL4 1XR. Tel: 01753 731005

Professional Golfers' Association – National HQ, Apollo House, The Belfry, Sutton Coldfield, West Midlands B76 9PT. Tel: 01675 470333. Publish a leaflet entitled *So you want to become a professional?*

RAC Motor Sports Association Ltd – Motor Sports House, Riverside Park, Coln Brook, Slough, Berks. SL3 0IIG. Tel: 01753 681736.

Royal Yachting Association – RYA House, Romsey Road, Eastleigh, Hampshire SO50 9YA. Tel: 01703 629962.

Careers in Sport, published by Kogan Page.
Working in Sport & Fitness, published by COIC.
Playing at the Top: a guide to professional sport, available from the CCPR, address as above.

Oceans of Opportunity describes a range of maritime career openings, and can be purchased from the Society of Underwater Technology – 76 Mark Lane, London EC3R 7JN. Tel: 0171 481 0750.

TEACHING SPORT

For details of training courses and application procedures, see the *Handbook of Initial Teacher Training*, published annually by NATFHE. This directory of teacher training courses is normally held in school, college and careers centre libraries.

British Association of Advisers and Lecturers in Physical Education – Nelson House, 6 The Beacon, Exmouth EX8 2AG. Tel: 01395 263247.

Teacher Training Agency – Communication Centre, PO Box 3210, Chelmsford. Tel: 01245 454454. Contact for a range of publications on teaching and teacher training.

Graduate Teacher Training Registry – Fulton House, Jessop Avenue, Cheltenham GL50 3SH. Tel: 01242 225868. Publishes a guide to PGCE courses and deals with postgraduate applications.

Physical Education Association of the United Kingdom (PEA UK) – Suite 5, 10 Churchill Square, Kingshill, West Malling, Kent ME19 4DU. Tel: 01732 875888. Can supply careers information on receipt of a stamped, addressed envelope.

A Career in Physical Education, Sport and Recreation, published by the Physical Education Association of the UK (address above).

PHYSIOTHERAPY AND SPORTS THERAPY

Chartered Society of Physiotherapy – 14 Bedford Row, London WC1R 4ED. Tel: 0171 242 1941 for information on physiotherapy training courses and entry requirements.

International Institute of Sports Therapy (part of Vocational Awards International) – 46 Aldwick Road, Bognor Regis, West Sussex, PO21 2PN. Tel: 01243 842064 for a list of institutions offering sports therapy courses.

Royal National Institute for the Blind (RNIB) – Physiotherapy Support Service Manager, 224 Great Portland Street, London W1N 6AA. Tel: 0171 388 1266.

Therapy Specialisms and Complementary Medicine, an AGCAS booklet.

DIVER TRAINING CENTRES

There are many places where you can receive training in diving, but the following training centres offer HSE-approved courses. The individual centres' prospectuses give details of the various courses on offer, and their entry requirements and fees.

Commercial Diving Centre – Dag House, Allens Lane, Poole, Dorset BH16 5DG. Tel: 01202 667111.

Fort Bovisand Underwater Centre – Plymouth Ocean Projects Ltd, 2 Fort Bovisand, Plymouth, Devon PL9 0AB. Tel: 01752 408021.

The Underwater Centre Ltd – Fort William, Inverness-shire PH33 6LZ. Tel: 01397 703786.

British Sub-Aqua Club – Telford's Quay, Ellesmere Port, South Wirral, Cheshire L46 4FY. Tel: 0151 357 1951. Can provide information sheets on careers in commercial and sport diving.

Health & Safety Executive – Safety Policy Division, Fifth Floor, South Side, Rose Court, 2 Southwark Bridge, London SE1 9HS. Tel: 0171 717 6592. Can supply the full list of HSE-approved diver training schools, some of which are attached to universities which offer courses in marine science.

LEISURE & RECREATION

Important note: *the inclusion of addresses of individuals and organisations in this book in no way guarantees their reputation. They are included as items of information only. All readers must judge for themselves whether organisations and training providers offer suitable courses, etc.*

Astrological Association of Great Britain – address as for the Urania Trust (see below). Tel: 0171 700 3746. Publishes *The Astrological Journal and Newsletter.*

Bingo Association of Great Britain – 4 St James Court, Wilderspool Causeway, Warrington, Cheshire WA4 6PS. Tel: 01925 234700.

British Actors' Equity Association – Upper St Martin's Lane, London WC2H 9EG. Tel: 0171 379 6000. (Has a section which looks after the interests of members who are variety entertainers and circus performers specifically.)

British Casino Association – 29 Castle Street, Reading, Berkshire RG1 7SL. Tel: 01734 589191.

Circomedia – Kingswood Foundation, Britannia Road, Kingswood, Bristol BS15 2DB. Tel: 0117 947 7288. Contact Kim Lawrence (administrator) for course details and their basic fund-raising package which advises students on how to find money for their fees, such as career development loans or the Skillsplus scheme.

Faculty of Astrological Studies – address as for the Urania Trust (see below). Tel: 0171 700 3566 for details of correspondence and other courses.

First Leisure Corporation – 7 Soho Street, London W1V 5FA. Tel: 0171 437 9727.

Horserace Totalisator Board – 74 Upper Richmond Road, Putney, London SW15 2SU. Tel: 0181 874 6411.

Institute of Leisure & Amenity Management – Education & Training Unit, ILAM House, Lower Basildon, Reading RG8 9NE. Tel: 01491 874222.

The Puppet Centre – BAC, Lavender Hill, London SW11 5TN. Tel: 0171 228 5335.

Rank Organisation – Group Personnel, York House, 45 Seymour Street, London W1H 6BB. Tel: 0171 706 1111.

Southern Games – 202 Fulham Road, Chelsea, London SW10 9NB. Tel: 0171 352 0034. (For trained and experienced croupiers only.)

Urania Trust – 396 Caledonian Road, London N1 1DN. Tel:

0171 700 0639. The Trust is an educational charity which encourages the study of astrology and acts as an umbrella organisation for other schools and organisations. Publishers of *Astrology 199– – the free guide to astrology worldwide.*

VIP International – VIP House, Charing Cross Road, London WC2H 0EP. Tel: 0171 930 0541.

Look in the GAN section of your careers library, and at further and higher education handbooks for details of relevant courses.

An AGCAS booklet for graduates – *Leisure and Hospitality Management* – may be available for consultation at careers libraries, and in some schools and colleges, or for purchase from CSU, Despatch Department, Armstrong House, Oxford Road, Manchester M1 7ED. Tel: 0161 236 9816, ext 250/251.

Directory of Leisure Courses in Higher Education, published by ILAM.

Working in Leisure and *Working in Tourism,* both published by COIC.

CAREERS FOR MUSICIANS

BBC Corporate Recruitment Services – PO Box 7000, London W12 7ZY. Tel: 0181 749 7000.

British Phonographic Industry – 25 Saville Row, London W1X 1AA. Tel: 0171 287 4422. For enquiries on all aspects of the record industry.

British Society for Music Therapy – 25 Rosslyn Avenue, East Barnet, Herts, EN4 8DH. Tel: 0181 368 8879.

Incorporated Society of Musicians (ISM) – 10 Stratford Place, London W1N 9AE. Tel: 0171 629 4413.

Music Publishers' Association Ltd – 3rd Floor, Strandgate, 18–20 York Buildings, London WC2N 6JU. Tel: 0171 839 7779.

Musicians' Union – 60/62 Clapham Road, London SW9 0JJ. Tel: 0171 582 5566.

National Music and Disability Information Service – Foxhole, Totnes, Devon TQ9 6EB. Tel: 01803 866701.

Schools of music include:

Birmingham Conservatoire – Paradise Place, Birmingham B3 3HG. Tel: 0121 331 5901.

City of Leeds College of Music – Cookridge Street, Leeds LS2 8BH. Tel: 0113 2452 069.

Guildhall School of Music & Drama – The Barbican, London EC2Y 8DT. Tel: 0171 628 2571.

London College of Music – Thames Valley University, St Mary's Road, Ealing W5 5RF. Tel: 0181 231 2304

Royal Academy of Music – Marylebone Road, London NW1 5HT. Tel: 0171 873 7373.

Royal College of Music – Prince Consort Road, London SW7 2BS. Tel: 0171 589 3643.

Royal Northern College of Music – 124 Oxford Road, Manchester M13 9RD. Tel: 0161 273 6283.

Royal School of Church Music – Addington Palace, Croydon, Surrey CR9 5AD. Tel: 0181 654 7676.

Royal Scottish Academy of Music and Drama – 100 Renfrew Street, Glasgow G2 3DB. Tel: 0141 332 4101

Trinity College of Music – 11 Mandeville Place, London W1M 6AQ. Tel: 0171 935 5773.

Welsh College of Music and Drama – Castle Grounds, Cathays Park, Cardiff CF1 3ER. Tel: 01222 342854 (for Neath College).

The *British Music Education Yearbook*, published by Rhinegold Publishing, includes a list of courses.

Music Teachers' Yearbook and *The Musicians' Handbook*, available from Rhinegold Publishing.

Careers with Music, available free from the Incorporated Society of Musicians (address above).

The First 10 Years (an information sheet for performers) and *Approaching an Agent*, published by ISM. This organisation would appreciate it if you could send a label with your name and address on it, when requesting publications.

Music Journal, published monthly: contact ISM for subscription details.

British Actors' Equity Association – Guild House, Upper St Martin's Lane, London WC2H 9EG. Tel: 0171 379 6000.

British Council of Ballroom Dancing – Terpsichore House, 240 Merton Road, South Wimbledon, London SW19 1EQ. Tel: 0181 545 0085.

College of the Royal Academy of Dancing – 36 Battersea Square, London SW11 3RA. Tel: 0171 223 0091.

Council for Dance Education & Training (UK) – Riverside Studios, Crisp Road, London W6 9RL. Tel: 0181 741 5084. Will provide general information and a list of accredited courses on receipt of a stamped, addressed envelope.

Foundation for Community Dance – 13–15 Belvoir Street, Leicester LE1 6SL.

Imperial Society of Teachers of Dancing – Imperial House, 22–26 Paul Street, London EC2A 4QE. Tel: 0171 837 9967.

International Dance Teachers' Association – International House, 76 Bennett Road, Brighton BN2 5JL. Tel: 01273 685652.

Laban Centre for Movement and Dance – Laurie Grove, New Cross, London SE14 6NH. Tel: 0181 692 4070.

London College of Dance – 10 Linden Road, Bedford MK40 2DA. Tel: 01234 213331.

London Contemporary Dance School – 17 Dukes Road, London WC1H 9AB. Tel: 0171 387 0152.

National Resource Centre for Dance – University of Surrey, Guildford GU2 5XH. Tel: 01483 259316. Publishes a directory on dance courses in higher education, *Dance Education, Training & Careers*.

DRAMA AND ACTING

British Actors' Equity Association – Guild House, Upper St Martin's Lane, London WC2H 9EG. Tel: 0171 379 6000.

Conference of Drama Schools – c/o The Central School of Speech and Drama, Embassy Theatre, Eton Avenue, London NW3 3HY. Tel: 0171 722 8183. Produces a useful annual *Guide to Courses*.

National Council for Drama Training – 5 Tavistock Place, London WC1H 9SN. Tel: 0171 387 3650. Send a stamped, addressed envelope for list of accredited courses.

Teacher Training Agency – Communication Centre, PO Box 3210, Chelmsford, Essex CM1 3WA. Tel: 01245 454454. Contact for publications on training to teach English and drama.

Careers in the Theatre, published by Kogan Page.

Working in Performing Arts, published by COIC.

The Stage is a weekly newspaper, available from your newsagent or on subscription from 47 Bermondsey Street, London SE1 3XT. Tel: 0171 403 1818.

Contacts – an annual directory of courses, venues, agents, contacts and events in the world of theatre and entertainment, published by Spotlight, 7 Leicester Place, London WC2H 7BP. Tel: 0171 437 7631.

Look through the *Times Educational Supplement*, which is published on Fridays, to get an idea of advertised vacancies for teachers.

BACKSTAGE THEATRE WORK

Arts Council Drama Department – 14 Great Peter Street, London SW1P 3NQ. Tel: 0171 333 0100.

Association of British Theatre Technicians – 47 Bermondsey Street, London SE1 3XT. Tel: 0171 403 3778. Produces a directory of courses and training opportunities; also a free leaflet on opportunities in backstage theatre work (send a stamped, addressed C5 envelope).

Royal Academy of Dramatic Art – 62–4 Gower Street, London WC1E 6ED. Tel: 0171 636 7076.

Spotlight – 7 Leicester Place, London WC2H 7BP. Tel: 0171 437 7631. Publishes *Contacts* – an annual list of information on companies, courses and everything to do with theatre work.

Stage Management Association – Southbank House, Black Prince Road, London SE1 7SJ. Tel: 0171 587 1514.

The Stage – weekly from newsagents.

British Theatre Directory is a useful source of theatre-related information available from Richmond House Publishing Company, Richmond Mews, London W1V 5AG. Tel: 0171 437 9556. This volume may be held in your local library.

THEATRE & ARTS ADMINISTRATION
The Arts Council of England – 14 Great Peter Street, London SW1P 3NQ. Tel: 0171 333 0100.

Spotlight, 7 Leicester Place, London WC2H 7BP. Tel: 0171 437 7631 for further details.

Theatre Works – a guide to working in the theatre is a useful booklet with a detailed section on administrative work in the theatre, produced by the Royal National Theatre's education and publication department. Contact the Royal National Theatre, c/o Bookshop, South Bank, London SE1 9PX. Tel: 0171 928 2033 ext. 600.

CREATIVE THERAPIES
When writing to these organisations, please enclose a stamped, addressed envelope.

Association of Dance Therapists (International) – 19 Ashlake Road, Streatham, London SW16 2BB.

British Association of Art Therapists – 11a Richmond Road, Brighton, Sussex BN2 3RL.

British Association for Dramatherapists – 5 Sunnydale Villas, Durlston Road, Swanage, Dorset BH19 2HY.

British Society for Music Therapy – 25 Rosslyn Avenue, East Barnet, Herts EN4 8DH. Tel: 0181 368 8879.

Rudolf Steiner Organisation – 35 Park Road, London NW1 6XT. Tel: 0171 724 7699.

GRAPHOLOGY
British Institute of Graphologists – 24–26 High Street, Hampton Hill, Middlesex TW12 1PD. Tel: 01753 891241.

Graphology Society – 33 Bonningtons, Thriftwood, Hutton, Brentwood, Essex CM13 2TL.

International Graphology Association – (Tutorial Section), Stonedge, Dunkerton, Bath BA2 8AS. Tel: 01761 437809.